I0413879

EIR (ISSN 0273-6314) *is published weekly
(50 issues), by EIR News Service, Inc.,
P.O. Box 17390, Washington, D.C. 20041-0390.
(703) 777-9451*

European Headquarters: E.I.R. GmbH, Postfach
Bahnstrasse 9a, D-65205, Wiesbaden, Germany
Tel: 49-611-73650
Homepage: http://www.eirna.com
e-mail: eirna@eirna.com
Director: Georg Neudecker

Montreal, Canada: 514-461-1557

Denmark: EIR - Danmark, Sankt Knuds Vej 11,
basement left, DK-1903 Frederiksberg, Denmark.
Tel.: +45 35 43 60 40, Fax: +45 35 43 87 57. e-mail:
eirdk@hotmail.com.

Mexico City: EIR, Sor Juana Inés de la Cruz 242-2
Col. Agricultura C.P. 11360
Delegación M. Hidalgo, México D.F.
Tel. (5525) 5318-2301
eirmexico@gmail.com

Common Future for Mankind and a Renaissance of Classical Culture

Creating a Common Future For Mankind and a Renaissance Of Classical Culture

Schiller Institute International Conference
June 25-26, 2016, Berlin, Germany

June 28—The Schiller Institute's international two-day conference gathered more than 300 guests from 24 nations and four continents for an intense and profound dialogue on how to stop the immediate danger of world war, by creating instead a new paradigm of global cooperation and development, based on a dialogue of civilizations and the unique creativity of mankind. Conference participants were very highly alerted to the escalation of western geopolitical confrontation against Russia and China, and the danger of thermonuclear war, and passed a resolution calling for an immediate end to sanctions against Russia and Syria. To end the war and to reconstruct war-torn Syria and the greater region of Southwest Asia, was a key focus of the conference, during which Dr. Bouthaina Shaaban, member of the presidency of Syria, addressed the conference audience and engaged in a moving Q&A via live stream video now available at: www.newparadigm.schillerinstitute.com.

Conference participants were also invited to attend a "Musical Dialogue of Cultures," organized jointly by NICE e.V. and the Schiller-Institut e.V. as a public, free-admission concert in a community church. The Camerata Geminiani, the international chorus of the Schiller Institute, and others performed classical European music in the Verdi tuning, along with choirs presenting folk songs from Russia, Ukraine, and China, before an excited audience of close to 500 guests and 150 musicians. It became clear, that only by creating a new paradigm for mankind, a renaissance of beauty, based on the sharing and promoting of each civilization's highpoints of their respective cultures, can humanity be saved from the abyss.

The Conference Panels

The first conference panel of five speakers on "The strategic crisis is more dangerous than at the height of the Cold War" was addressed by Helga Zepp-La-Rouche, founder and president of the Schiller Institute; Chas Freeman, former U.S. ambassador to Saudi Arabia; Col. (ret.) Alain Corvez, former adviser to the French Defense and Interior Ministries; Lt. Col. (ret.) Ulrich Scholz, former fighter pilot, NATO planner, and lecturer on air warfare; and American economist and statesman Lyndon LaRouche.

Speaking on the second panel, "The Crisis of the Trans-Atlantic Financial System and How To Overcome It," were Jacques Cheminade, candidate in the French presidential elections; Marco Zanni, head of the M5S delegation in the Economic and Monetary Affairs Committee of the European Parliament; Daisuke Kotegawa, research director of the Canon Institute for Global Studies, Japan, and former representative of Japan to the IMF; and Leonidas Chrysanthopoulos, former Greek ambassador to Poland, Canada, and Armenia, and former secretary general of the Black Sea Economic Cooperation Organization.

The third panel, "The New Paradigm Represented by the 'One Belt, One Road' Policy," heard Dr. Ren Lin, researcher on the One Belt, One Road policy at the

Chinese Academy of Social Science; H.E. Hamid Sidig, ambassador and extraordinary representative of the Islamic Republic of Afghanistan to Germany; and Egbert Drews, board member of MARWIKO AG, Berlin.

Sunday's deliberations continued the "Silk Road—New Paradigm" panel with a strong emphasis on Syria and the need to end geopolitical confrontation and foreign-funded terrorism, and to create peace and prosperity in the region. After hearing her prepared video address on the situation in Syria, the audience had the extraordinary opportunity to engage in a moving, 30-minute live video dialogue with H.E. Dr. Bouthaina Shaaban of the Presidency of the Syrian Arab Republic, who asked everyone to bring about a new paradigm of creative human development ("an intellectual Silk Road") instead of war and destruction.

Michel Raimbaud—former French ambassador to Arab, African, and Latin American countries and former director of the French Office of Protection of Refugees and Stateless Persons—had opened Sunday's portion of the panel with a passionate plea to rebuild peace in accordance with international law, in Syria and everywhere else. Hussein Askary, *EIR* Arabic editor, presented a video on the reconstruction of Aleppo in the context of the New Silk Road, followed by a presentation by Prof. Talal Moualla of the board of trustees, The Syria Trust for Development, and executive director of the Syrian Cultural Heritage Transformation project of the Ministry of Culture in Syria. The panel was concluded by Bereket Simon, chairman of the Commercial Bank of Ethiopia and adviser to the Prime Minister of Ethiopia, and by a video message from Fouad al-Ghaffari, chairman of the Advisory Office for Coordination with the BRICS from the war-torn Republic of Yemen.

Speaking on the fourth panel, "The Frontiers Of Science: The New Economic Platform Based on a Fusion Economy and Man's Future in Space," were Adeline Djeutie, formerly with the International Atomic Energy Agency and now an independent consultant in Vienna; Alain Gachet, chairman of Radar Technologies International; and Rainer Sandau, technical director of Satellites and Space Applications of the International Academy of Astronautics.

After a classical musical introduction, violinist Gian Marco Sanna, founder and artistic director of the Geminiani Project, London, contributed a discussion on the importance of the scientific musical tuning of A = 432 Hz (the "Verdi tuning"), which the Schiller Institute has promoted for decades. Hussein Askary presented the "Elephant Clock" as an example of the beauty of the Islamic Renaissance and its connection to the ancient Silk Road.

The panelists then joined with Mrs. Zepp-LaRouche and Lyndon LaRouche for the concluding general discussion on how to secure a global collaboration for the common aims of mankind, by focussing on bringing forward the principle of creativity in each human individual, as the only way to stop the present mortal danger for civilization.

For more information, contact Mrs. Leona Meyer-Kasai, Schiller Institute Berlin, at konferenz2016@schiller-institut.de

EIR Contents

www.larouchepub.com Volume 43, Number 27, July 1, 2016

MARWIKO AG

Cover This Week

Left to right: Schiller Institute President Helga Zepp-LaRouche; Afghanistan's Ambassador to Germany H.E. Hamid Sidig; MARWIKO AG Board Member Egbert Drews; Ren Lin of the Chinese Academy of Social Sciences.

COMMON FUTURE FOR MANKIND AND A RENAISSANCE OF CLASSICAL CULTURE

2 FROM THE SCHILLER INSTITUTE
Creating a Common Future for Mankind & a Renaissance of Classical Culture

I. BERLIN SCHILLER INSTITUTE CONFERENCE

5 Conference Program
The detailed program as distributed at the conference

7 PANEL I
The Strategic Crisis Is 'More Dangerous than at the Height of the Cold War'

21 Discussion

27 PANEL II
The Crisis of the Trans-Atlantic Financial System and How To Overcome It

36 PANEL III
The New Paradigm Represented by the 'One Belt, One Road' Policy

54 PANEL IV
The Frontiers of Science: The New Economic Platform Based on a Fusion Economy and Man's Future in Space

58 PANEL V
The Positive Historical Traditions and Renaissance Periods Linking Europe to China, to Russia, to America, and to the Arab World

60 End of Conference Discussion

II. WHAT IS DEDICATION?

66 FIRESIDE CHAT WITH MICHAEL STEGER
Resolving Upward

Conference speeches and discussion not published in this issue will be published as soon as possible.

I. Berlin Schiller Institute Conference

Creating a Common Future for Mankind and A Renaissance of Classical Culture

June 25-26, 2016 – Berlin, Germany

Conference program

SATURDAY, JUNE 25

9:00 REGISTRATION

PANEL I: The strategic crisis is "more dangerous than at the height of the Cold War"

- Musical introduction: "Sheep May Safely Graze" from the Hunting Cantata BWV 208, J. S. Bach, arrangement for piano
Ya-ou Xie, China

- Keynote: The future of mankind will be beautiful – provided we can avoid the fate of the dinosaurs
Helga Zepp-LaRouche, President of the Schiller Institute

- Things fall apart: America, Europe, and Asia in the new world disorder
Chas Freeman, former U.S. ambassador to Saudi Arabia and main interpreter for Richard Nixon during his 1972 trip to China

- The enormous potential of a new paradigm for all of mankind
Vladimir Yakunin, Chairman, World Public Forum Dialogue of Civilizations

- Will the American hubris come to an end, or will it disappear with us in a universal combustion?
Col. (ret.) Alain Corvez, International consultant, former advisor to the French Defense and Interior Ministries

- War – a pathology of the West
Lt. Col. (ret.) Ulrich Scholz, former German fighter pilot, NATO planner and lecturer on air warfare

13:30-14:30 LUNCH BREAK

PANEL II: The crisis of the trans-Atlantic financial system and how to overcome it
14:30-16:00

- Keynote: The LaRouche method of physical economy
Jacques Cheminade, candidate in the French presidential elections

- The collapse of the European financial system and the failure of the banking union
Marco Zanni, Head of M5S delegation in the Economic and Monetary Affairs Committee of the European Parliament

- Japan's outlook concerning Eurasian cooperation
Daisuke Kotegawa, Canon Institute Japan, former representative of Japan to the IMF

- Global Crisis: Proposals for Solution
  Leonidas Chrysanthopoulos, former Greek Ambassador to Poland, Canada and Armenia, former Secretary General of the Black Sea Economic Cooperation Organisation (BSEC)

PANEL III: The new paradigm represented by the "One Belt, One Road" policy
16:00-18:00

- Opening remarks

- The New Silk Road win-win perspective
  Ren Lin, Researcher on the One Belt One Road Policy at Chinese Academy of Social Sciences (CASS)

- Greeting
  H.E. Hamid Sidig, Ambassador and Extraordinary Representative of the Islamic Republic of Afghanistan to Germany

- International networking in the economy: Practical experience
  Egbert Drews, board member of MARWIKO AG, Berlin

- Discussion

Classical concert: Musical dialogue of cultures
20:00 (Entrance at 19:30)

SUNDAY, JUNE 26

Continuation of Panel III
10:00-13:30

- Musical introduction: "Vecchio! spiccai da te...", recitative and arias of Francesco, opera "I masnadieri", Giuseppe Verdi
  Martino Hammerle-Bortolotti, Baritone, and Helena Fialová, Piano

- In Syria and elsewhere, against the war party and the law of the jungle, rebuild peace in accordance with law
  Michel Raimbaud, Former French ambassador particularly in the Arab world, in Africa and Latin America. Former Director of the French Office of Protection of Refugees and Stateless Persons (OFPRA)

- Reconstruction with Syrian characteristics: rebuilding a truly diverse and more secure world based on the lessons of the Syrian experience
  Her Excellency Dr. Bouthaina Shaaban, Presidency of the Syrian Arab Republic

- The reconstruction of Aleppo (Video)

- Repositioning of the cultural variable: Towards a new modern cultural approach
  Talal Moualla, Board of Trustees, The Syria Trust for

Development, Executive director of "Syrian Cultural Heritage Transformation" project – Ministry of Culture, Syria

- Message to the Schiller Institute Conference from The Yemeni Advisory Office for Coordination with the BRICS (Video)
  Fouad Al-Ghaffari, Chairman of the Advisory Office for Coordination with the BRICS, Sanaa, Republic of Yemen

- A win-win cooperation with Africa
  Bereket Simon, chairman of the Commercial Bank of Ethiopia and advisor to the Prime Minister

13:30-14:30 Lunch break

Panel IV: The frontiers of science: the new economic platform based on a fusion economy and man's future in space
14:30-15:45

- Opening remarks

- How new space technologies can change the groundwater geopolitical balance : case studies in Kenya and Iraq
  Alain Gachet, Chairman of Radar Technologies International, France

- Towards a New Era of International Space Cooperation
  Rainer Sandau, Technical Director, Satellites and Space Applications, of the International Academy of Astronautics (IAA)

- Sustaining energy development in developing and emerging countries: What role could nuclear energy play?
  Adeline Djeutie, Independent Consultant, Vienna

PANEL V: The positive historical traditions and Renaissance periods linking Europe to China, to Russia, to America, and to the Arab world
15:45-18:00

- Musical introduction: Korean folk song "Dear mother, dear sister", Sowol Kim; "Das Veilchen", W.A. Mozart, Goethe
  Sua Baek, Soprano, Korea – Benjamin Lylloff, Piano, Denmark

- Opening remarks

- The Verdi tuning: a demonstration
  Gian Marco Sanna, Violinist, founder and artistic director of The Geminiani Project, London

- Beauty of the Islamic Renaissance: the elephant clock
  Hussein Askary

- Panel Discussion with Conference Participants

CONFERENCE RESOLUTION

The Strategic Crisis Is 'More Dangerous Than at the Height of the Cold War'

HELGA ZEPP-LAROUCHE

Mankind's Beautiful Future—If We Avoid the Dinosaurs' Fate

Zepp-LaRouche, President of the Schiller Institute in Germany, gave the conference keynote address on June 25, entitled, "The Future of Mankind Will Be Beautiful—Provided We Can Avoid the Fate of the Dinosaurs." This is an edited transcript.

Ladies and gentlemen, distinguished guests, dear friends of the Schiller Institute: I think we all have come to this conference because everybody who is in this room knows that we are experiencing an absolutely unprecedented, systemic and existential crisis of civilization. We have the coincidence of a war danger, where NATO is confronting Russia in a very, very aggressive fashion—which could lead to a Third World War. We have a U.S. confrontation against China

EIRNS/Julien Lemaître

Founder of the Schiller Institutes, Helga Zepp-LaRouche, delivering the keynote address to the June 25, 2016 Schiller Institute conference in Berlin, Germany.

in the South China Sea. We have the danger of a new 2008 type of financial crisis, which could blow up the financial system, and naturally we had, two days ago, the Brexit—Great Britain voting to leave the European Union. And as we all know, this was not a vote against Europe as such, but it was a vote against a completely unjust system and a corrupt elite.

This conference has one topic, or one subsuming topic, and that is to define solutions to these crises: to discuss what would be the new paradigm, and is mankind capable of solving such an existential crisis?

We have distinguished speakers from four continents, from many countries, and obviously these are the people, or they are representative of the kinds of people, who are determined that a solution is to be found.

Before I go these various mortal dangers, the solution is easy. So be at rest and calm. If mankind unites for a good plan and acts in solidarity with courage, any crisis in human civilization can be overcome, because that is the nature of human beings—that when we are challenged with a great evil, an even greater force of good is awakened in our soul.

Now, look at the situation. Great Britain voted on Thursday by 52% to leave the EU. Immediately you had an explosion in the financial markets in the morning hours of Friday—£5 trillion were wiped out. It could have been Black Friday. The turbulences continue. So some people are now in absolute dismay, saying, "how could we be so wrong? The bookmakers were telling us until midnight the opposite, that everything would be fine. How did we get caught on such a wrong foot?"

Now I will talk about that, but let me preface it by saying that maybe this Brexit is a blessing in disguise. Because it is a vote against a supranational bureaucracy, a soulless Brussels dictatorship. It's a vote against robbery of national sovereignty, against a completely heartless European Union Commission, which has been completely alienated from the people in Europe, a European Union which has no unity. It has no humanity. And the Brexit creates the opportunity to build a completely new Europe.

The *Erinyes*

I remember at a Schiller Conference in 2003—this was the day the Iraq War started—I prefaced my speech by saying, "Are these people insane? Don't they know that, by attacking a country on the basis of lies, they will call forth the *Erinyes*, those goddesses of natural law, who may not act immediately—but there is a higher justice which corrects things." And I find it a historical irony, if you will, the connection between the British voting against the EU membership, and the connection to the illegal war against Iraq. Remember that it was the Iraq war that was one of the root causes of the refugee crisis, one of the root causes of Europe being in such distress, and now, of all people, the British people are voting something which is the destruction of the British Empire, and may lead from a Great Britain to a very tiny Britain, namely if Scotland and Ireland leave. I think this is a higher justice, and the proof that nemesis *is* a force in history.

Let me focus on the underlying danger, which is not eliminated by this, but, as I said, it creates new open-

screen grab/RT

Prof. Stephen F. Cohen, Russian expert at NYU and Princeton.

ings to find a solution.

The Powderkeg

We are sitting on a powder keg, and any of the different strategic crises right now could be the trigger of a thermonuclear war. There are many people—not many, but at least some people, military experts primarily—who have said that we are now in a situation which is more dangerous than during the height of the Cold War. That was naturally the Cuban Missile Crisis. After this war danger had been present for a variety of reasons for a long time, only in the most recent days have people suddenly begun to speak about it. German Foreign Minister Frank-Walter Steinmeier—he talks about the NATO maneuvers in the Baltics as war cries and saber-rattling. Wolfgang Ischinger, head of the Munich Security Conference and a staunch Atlanticist, says there is the danger of an escalation into a military confrontation. NATO must tame itself. *NATO must tame itself*, he says.

Gernot Erler, Germany's Special Coordinator for Russia Policy, says NATO is escalating the situation up to a war; it should stop. Professor Steven F. Cohen, a Russia expert at New York University and Princeton: The United States is the biggest threat to the world, and if the Obama administration were to do what the 51 State Department dissenters who just published an open letter to Obama said—namely to topple Assad—within a short period of time ISIS would sit in Damascus, and the United States would be involved in a war with Syria, Iran, and Russia.

Then you have, between now and the July NATO Summit in Warsaw, five NATO maneuvers at the Russian border in Poland and the Baltic countries, involving between 50,000 to 60,000 troops combined. Simultaneously the United States is moving aircraft carrier strike groups into the Mediterranean, warships of the Aegis class into the Black Sea, and other U.S. warships into the Baltic Sea. Four battalions will be put in the Baltic countries after the Warsaw Summit. There is a full arms race going on, with modernization of all nuclear arsenals on both sides. The same dynamic with different predicates is essentially happening around the South China Sea, between the United States and China.

There was no problem in the South China Sea until the government of the Philippines, in a clear violation of international law—that is, the previous Philippines government—pushed by the United States, took the territorial dispute to the Court of Arbitration in The Hague. The United States, under the pretext of freedom of navigation of the seas, is now continuously violating the 12-mile zone, overflying Chinese islands and reefs, and the propaganda line for both—the two conflicts, with Russia and China—is that Russia illegally occupied Crimea, and that China is involved in aggressive land-grabbing of islands in the South China Sea. And that all the moves by the United States and NATO are only in response to the aggressive behavior of Russia and China.

That is a complete lie. The question to start from is, How is it that 71 years after World War II ended, when a world in ruins made a solemn commitment "never again," "never again genocide," "never again war,"— how is it that 25 years after the disintegration of the Soviet Union, we are now at the verge of World War III?

The Promise

There are new transcripts now available that show very clearly that in the period between 1989 and 1991, there was a series of meetings in which the United States gave a clear promise to the Soviet Union to not expand NATO to the borders of Russia. On February 9, 1990, then Secretary of State James Baker said that if Germany were unified as part of the West, and joined NATO, then the United States will give "an iron-clad guarantee that NATO will not expand one inch eastward."

This was the key element in why Soviet President Gorbachov agreed to the unification talks. Sure, there was no formal deal made, but there are many eyewitnesses, former U.S. Ambassador to Moscow Jack Matlock and others, who say that Baker gave the promise on

EIRNS/Stuart Lewis

President H.W. Bush, Soviet Foreign Minister Eduard Shevardnadze, and U.S. Secretary of State James Baker in Washington, D.C. on Sept. 21, 1989.

May 18, 1990, that the United States will cooperate with the Soviet Union for the development of a new Europe. In June 1990 Bush promised Soviet leaders that the United States would work toward an inclusive Europe.

Now it is clear that, at the same time that these promises were given, the neocons in the United States were working on the Project for a New American Century (PNAC) doctrine. It declared that with the collapse of the Soviet Union, the United States would insist on a unipolar world: namely, that it would not allow any nation, or any group of nations, ever to surpass the power of the United States, economically or politically.

In the middle of the 1990s, East European countries, former members of the Warsaw Pact—Poland, Hungary, the Czech Republic, the Baltic nations, and others— were ushered into NATO. Yeltsin, Medvedev, and Gorbachov protested against this, both privately and publicly. The United States violated the no-eastward-expansion agreements with Russia and went for regime change. Victoria Nuland admitted publicly that the State Department spent $5 billion on the color revolution in Ukraine alone. Helmut Schmidt, the late Chancellor of Germany, said that the Ukraine crisis started with the EU Maastricht agreement, because that was the moment when the EU turned into an empire with the idea to endlessly gain new members, and that EU eastward expansion occurred in parallel with NATO eastward expansion.

The Ukraine Crisis

What triggered the Ukraine crisis, and therefore the crisis with Russia—which was already building,— but what formally triggered it, was an event at the Vilnius EU summit in late 2013. The EU proposed to establish the Eastern Partnership project and associate Ukraine with the EU. At the last moment, Ukrainian President Yanukovych recognized that that would give NATO access to Ukraine, and would open Russia to all European Union products, and that would be ruinous for the Russian economy. So he opted out at the last moment, and then you had the activation of the NGOs, financed by the State Department; you had the activation of the Ukrainian Nazis in the tradition of Stepan Bandera.

This led to the coup on February 22, 2014, and the referendum in the Crimea. It was not an annexation by Russia; it was a referendum by the majority of the people of Crimea, occurring in reaction to the fascist coup in Kiev. And that record has to be set straight, because unless we look at that chronology, we will be entrapped by the war propaganda that is leading to World War III.

Defendants at the trial at Nuremberg.

NATO's Prompt Global Strike

Now, in the meantime, quite some years ago, the NATO doctrine was changed from Mutually Assured Destruction—which was the idea that nobody could use nuclear weapons because it would lead to the annihilation of mankind—to the utopian conception of a winnable, limited nuclear war. That is the basis for NATO's current Prompt Global Strike. This is the logic behind the establishment of the U.S. anti-ballistic missile system worldwide. That that system does not have the function to protect against Iranian missiles, should have been clear after the successful P5+1 agreement with Iran. That idea of a winnable first strike is also the logic behind the Air Sea Battle doctrine against China.

The same Obama who promised in 2009 that he would work to get a nuclear-free world, has committed $1 trillion for the modernization of all U.S. nuclear arsenals, such as the B61-12 warhead, of which there are probably 200 stationed in European countries. The idea is that these modernized tactical nuclear weapons are more usable, because you can put them on stealth bombers, and break through the air defenses of your opponent. So that's the case with the long-range stand-off weapons, the LRSW.

Sen. Dianne Feinstein and Undersecretary for Arms Control and International Security Ellen Tauscher—in their open letter in the *New York Times* several weeks ago—wrote that these weapons systems should not be built, because they greatly increase the danger of nuclear war by blurring the line between conventional and nuclear weapons. The whole idea, in this day and age, to build new nuclear weapons is unnecessary, costly, and dangerous, they say, and I would say it is criminal, because it is part of preparing a war of aggression which, in the Nuremberg Tribunal, was declared to be the highest crime against humanity.

Time to Leave NATO

So that's the situation. And the thing that drives me absolutely crazy, is that you have a situation which is more dangerous than during the Cold War Cuban Missile Crisis for a variety of reasons—because it involves thermonuclear weapons, the code of behavior between NATO and the East has broken down, there is no red telephone between Obama and Putin—so despite that, the public is sleeping! The people are sleepwalking again into world war, as they did in going into World War I. And one of the purposes of this conference is to change that, and get a public debate from our standpoint that *we do not want to be part of this*.

That is why I have called—and our colleagues in other countries have called—for governments to recognize that now is the time to leave NATO. I have not done that in the past, despite criticism, but when you have a clear danger that a continuation of this policy pursued by NATO right now, could lead to the extinction of mankind, I think it is only possible to give one answer: *Get out of an organization which is involved in criminal preparation of world war.* [applause]

Financial Armageddon

There is a second existential crisis which we all know: the immediate possibility of a crash of the trans-Atlantic financial system. Wells Fargo, Bank of America, and others are involved in the same practices as in 2008, by giving subprime mortgage loans. The too-big-to-fail banks all have gigantic bubbles in shale and oil gas. They have bubbles in other areas—cars.

LaRouche PAC anti-NATO organizing in New York City in 2016.

The only difference from 2008 is that all the instruments of the central banks have been used up. Lowering interest rates? Well, you can make it even lower,— negative interest rates. You can make people pay 10% to even deposit their money in the banks, which is almost what is happening. So, many businesses do not put their money in banks any more; they keep it either under their mattresses, or in their safes, or wherever. And then there is the idea of printing helicopter money; in response to the Brexit crisis, the Federal Reserve, the European Central Bank, and the Bank of England are working 24 hours around the clock to decide how much helicopter money they have to print to prevent a collapse of the system.

New Silk Road

That is just the end of it, and we have to come to grips with the fact that this system is absolutely finished. Now that, as I said, is no reason to despair, because the Brexit opens the way to join a completely new strategic system. The Schiller Institute has campaigned since 2013, when President Xi Jinping announced the New Silk Road, that that approach must become a global program for reconstruction for the world economy, and we published a study called *The New Silk Road Becomes the World Land-Bridge.*

Look at what has happened since the announcement of the New Silk Road: In less than three years, this new system has developed an enormous dynamic. Now 70 countries are participating in the Asian Infrastructure Investment Bank (AIIB), a banking system associated with the New Silk Road. By the end of the year, it is expected that 100 countries will have joined this new system; 18 countries are already part of the Shanghai Cooperation Organization (SCO), which overlaps the BRICS and the New Silk Road. There are new banking systems, the AIIB, the New Development Bank, the Shanghai Cooperation Bank, the Maritime Silk Road Fund, the Silk Road Fund, the SAARC bank—that's the bank for the South Asian Association for Regional Cooperation.

And the Silk Road is progressing quickly. There are at present seven or eight new train connections between China and Europe, from Chengdu, Xi'an, Chongqing, Yiwu, and Lianyungang, to such places as Madrid, Lyon, Herne, Duisburg, Hamburg, and Rotterdam, and the number is growing. President Xi Jinping has been in the Czech Republic, in Poland, in Serbia, in Germany and France; everywhere he has been, the idea of cooperation with China and the New Silk Road has become a powerful dynamic. The President of Switzerland went to China. Austria wants to become a hub of the New Silk Road. Greece is joining the Maritime Silk Road— China is building up the port of Piraeus near Athens. Now China is building a rail connection between Budapest and Belgrade, which eventually will link up with the Maritime Silk Road at Piraeus by bringing more goods this way.

President Pranab Mukherjee of India was in China and spoke very, very bravely about the India-China strategic partnership, so all this talk about big tensions between India and China—forget it, it's all Western propaganda.

When President Xi Jinping was in Iran, it was agreed that the Silk Road will extend to Iran. Shortly thereafter, Prime Minister Narendra Modi was in Iran, together with the President of Afghanistan, Ashraf Ghani, and they discussed not only the building the port of Chabahar—which will be a crucial element of the Silk Road, eventually going to India—but also Afghanistan's desire to be a hub for building the Silk Road between China and Europe; in that way, Afghanistan will be reconstructed.

In 2013 Xi Jinping invited all the countries of the world to join in the "win-win cooperation"; President Putin has offered, many times, the integration of Europe from the Atlantic to the Pacific, from Vladivostok to Lisbon.

What Happened to the EU?

OK, so how do we look at this situation, and how do we come forward? What spirit and what historical precedent is necessary to make it possible for European nations to enter into alliance with the Eurasian Economic Union and participation in the One Belt, One Road policy—to enter a new geometry?

Well, first of all, we have to start with the realization that the EU, as it developed from the Adenauer-de Gaulle conception as a political union of na-

Xinhua/Zheng Bin
Chinese and French officials posing in front of the first freight train from Wuhan, China to Lyon, France, a 11,300 kilometer journey which passed through five other countries before arriving in France.

Indian President Shri Pranab Mukherjee (right), with China President Xi Jinping, inspecting the Guard of Honor at the welcome ceremony in Beijing on May 26, 2016.

tion-states, and as it was expressed in the original Elysée Treaty between Adenauer and de Gaulle, did not survive. When it was unfortunately modified in 1963 by means of a preamble, the modified EU then led directly to the Maastricht/Lisbon EU, and that model is *over*.

It has failed, and considering the disgusting behavior of the [EU] Troika against Greece and other southern European countries, but especially how the EU dealt with the refugee crisis, you can see the complete moral collapse of Brussels. There is no more Schengen, it's over! If you have barbed wire along the borders of the Balkan countries, there is no more open travelling within Europe, there is no unity within the European Union, no solidarity, and no solutions and no visions.

The EU deal with Turkish President Recep Erdogan, to give this guy who's financing ISIS to the present day, $6 billion, so that he can keep people in camps to prevent them from reaching Europe—and with no guarantees for the rights of these refugees—is absolutely disgusting and a violation of human rights. [applause] Doctors Without Borders was absolutely correct in refusing to accept any money from the EU because of this behavior.

The emergence of right-wing populist to outright fascist organizations in Europe *is* the result of the failure of the European elites and their submission to the EU dictatorship.

Ambrose Evans-Prit-

DaD/Bundesbildstelle

French President Charles de Gaulle (left), meets German Federal Chancellor Konrad Adenauer during a visit to Germany in 1961. The leaders signed a treaty that reconciled the French and German peoples to each other.

chard, an MI5 mouthpiece in the *Daily Telegraph*, wrote a while ago that this EU of Brussels is exactly carrying out British policy. And what we are seeing in the EU is what Churchill always wanted. He wanted a united Europe, but with the British outside, so it could manipulate Europe from the outside, and then run the world on the basis of the special Anglo-American relationship.

In the summer of 1962, after Adenauer went to France and after the fantastic journey of de Gaulle to Germany, where he was greeted with absolute love and admiration, the two of them proposed a union without Great Britain. De Gaulle asked Adenauer, Are you prepared to work with France, if need be only our two countries? And Adenauer answered with a clear "Yes." The union was the real goal of the Elysée Treaty of Jan. 22, 1963, and before that, of the Fouchet Plan. But unfortunately, de Gaulle and Adenauer lost the fight with the Atlanticists in the German Bundestag, and the Gaullists were outvoted in France. Adenauer at that time was already weakened, because Ludwig Erhard had already been designated as his successor.

Then, on May 16, 1963, a preamble was forced through, which had the following elements: a close partnership with the United States; a common defense in NATO; Great Britain joining the European Economic Commission; a free-trade agreement, GATT. So the Atlanticists won, and that was the lost chance of Europe leading to the present crisis.

It led to a very rocky road, but it is very clear that Europe must find some form of working together, and obviously, the City of London and Wall Street, which has always been a British *dépendance*, they are deadly opposed to such a solution.

Go Back to de Gaulle-Adenauer

Klaus von Dohnanyi, the former German Minister of Education under Chancellor Willy Brandt from 1972 and 1974, in a very interesting June 17 article in the *Frankfurter Allgemeine Zeitung*, discussed exactly this Adenauer-de Gaulle cooperation and that the original Europe Economic Community did not include Great Britain and had no clear integration into NATO structures. Nor did the European Commission or European Parliament have any real responsibility.

It was the idea of a European fatherland of fatherlands; it was Germany, France, Italy, Belgium, Netherlands, and Luxemburg. De Gaulle wanted this European political union of sovereign states, and he was concerned that in any case, if it came to a serious crisis, the United States would only pursue its own interests in Europe.

Klaus von Dohnanyi, in this article, writes that he, as the leader of a NATO exercise in 1979, found that upon the first Soviet advance into German territory, the United States used tactical nuclear weapons on German territory with no previous announcement; and that, by the way, was the situation in the entire Cold War period, and everybody who has studied the matter knows that. So that is essentially the situation today, as well.

But even in 1950, Adenauer said in a famous inter-

German Federal Archive/Harald Hoffmann

Klaus von Dohnanyi at the April 20, 1982 SPD Party Conference in Munich.

view with Kingsbury Smith, that a union between Germany and France would give significant new life and a powerful fresh impetus to the European idea. Dohnanyi says that even Helmut Schmidt, who supported the preamble at first, recognized in 1983 that it was a big mistake, and that without an alliance of Germany and France there can be no progress in Europe.

So, can the German government, in light of the totally muddled situation, undertake such an initiative today? Dohnanyi says yes, it can, but the debate must come from the rank and file of society and the parties. The German-French alliance remains Europe's destiny, but the only way to overcome the pessimistic mood in Europe is to go back to the two most courageous men after 1945—de Gaulle and Adenauer.

It is perhaps a coincidence, but Foreign Minister Steinmeier has invited the six founding EU members to a summit in Berlin: Germany, France, Italy, and the Benelux countries. They say it was planned a long time ago, but I think this is very interesting.

Cusa and Confucius: New Paradigm

Now, having this historical frame of reference in mind, let's look at the epistemological basis for a new paradigm. How can we get society to join in serving the common aims of mankind, to agree to rise above geopolitics and join in a global development partnership? Well, who is right? Is it those who say that geopolitical conflict must always exist, chauvinism against other countries is OK, xenophobia against other nations, even hatred against other ethnic groups? Well, I'll tell you, the problem is that these people are thinking on a lower level, namely, on the level of sense-perception or Aristotelian logic and contradictions.

To save mankind, we need a completely different level of thinking and I would like, for this purpose, to turn to Nicholas of Cusa, who was probably the most

portrait, Gentile Bellini

Portrait of Great Sultan Mehmet II, 1480.

passionate proponent of an understanding among peoples, as an expression of the relation between the One and the Many, for which he developed a revolutionary, new method of thinking, which he called the *coincidentia oppositorum*, the coincidence of opposites.

For Cusa, nations—characterized by their languages—have natural and inalienable rights, because they are legitimate as nations, but they are united through what he called the *spiritus universorum*—the universal spirit—discussed in his book, *De Docta Ignorantia* (On Learned Ignorance), which is efficient in the entire universe. "Nations are expressions of diversity and specificity, but their unity exists before their diversity." This you find also in Confucius, who says, "there is unity in diversity."

Nicholas says, "the whole universe precedes all other things as that which coincides the most perfectly, corresponding to the order of nature, so that each participates in everything. *Quod libet in quo libet.*" Concretely this means that each nation can be integrated into a higher, inclusive order without losing its characteristics, because the unity is already in existence before the multitude.

Clash of Civilizations, 1453

For Nicholas, there is one humanity, in which all national expressions are of a lower significance. In his famous *Sermon 204*, he says, "The light-skinned German and the dark-skinned Ethiopian are equally human beings." Nicholas was no stranger to other nations. He travelled through almost every European nation; he travelled to Constantinople. When Mehmet II took over Constantinople in 1453, people experienced it as a tremendous clash of civilizations, but Cusa responded with the beautiful ecumenical dialogue, *De Pace Fidei* (On the Peace of the Faith), about peace and religion. Its essential idea is that all religious leaders and all philosophers of all nations can agree that there is only one truth, one God, and one religion, or as Confucius would say, "one harmony."

"Concordance is the highest form of truth," Nicholas says in the *Concordantia Catholica* (Universal Concord). An understanding between different nations and religions is possible because they can all produce universal discoveries which can be replicated and recognized by all others.

In Cusa's *The Layman on Experiments Done with Weight-Scales*, he says that all discoveries made by one country must immediately be made available internationally, so that all others can access what had been hidden.

Nicholas consciously broke with the axioms and the popular beliefs of the Middle Ages, with what was taught in the universities among educated elites, which was Scholasticism and the doctrines of the Peripatetics, people believing only in logic and contradictions.

Higher than 'Understanding'

Nicholas regarded the level of the senses and of understanding only as tools to put things in order. But on that level, nothing new will ever be created. The creation of the new can only occur on the level of reason, by thinking from above, thinking from a higher level, where the contradictions of the lower level are resolved. In the human intellect lies an indestructible prior knowledge, because, he says, if we did not have it, we would never seek something new, and if we discovered something, we would not know that what we found was what we had sought. Because this prior knowledge is not the result of deduction, but is really a form of intuition, of prescience, and it leads to the creativity of discovery of true universal principles in science and Classical art.

Now, all human beings have a natural condition, a mettle for humanity, and in most cultures there are teachings for how to reach that level of creativity and reason, and how to overcome the barbarism of uneducated emotions and logical thinking. In Confucius there is a demand for eternal learning and self-perfection. Each human being should have the aspiration to become a *junzi*, a noble person devoted to the common good.

Schiller's and Ehricke's Citizenship

In European humanism, Friedrich Schiller in my view has the deepest and most inspiring program for the perfection of mankind through aesthetical education. He proposes to educate the emotions up to the level of reason, so that each person eventually can become a beautiful soul, for whom freedom and necessity, duty and passion, are the same thing. For Schiller, universal history encompasses all humanity. The torch of culture and qualitative advancement is sometimes carried by this nation, then by that culture, but they all have potential for development, to reach a condition of world citizenship in which all original potentials of the human species will be developed.

Schiller says, "The boundaries are breached which isolated states and nations in hostile egoism. All thinking minds are now bound together by the bond of world citizenship, and all the light of the century can now illuminate the spirit of a new Galileo and a new Erasmus."

I think mankind is exactly at that point: We are at the beginning of a new era, which is within reach if we act in the right way. Mankind can reach what Krafft Ehricke called the "extraterrestrial imperative," meaning that man can become adult. Ehricke, the German rocket scientist, had a beautiful vision of space colonization as the next natural phase of evolution in the universe.

He developed very beautifully how evolution has occurred over long spans, how the development of life moved from the oceans to land; how, with the help of photosynthesis, plant life emerged on Earth; how, from amphibians and reptiles, evolution jumped to mammals, and finally to human beings; how human beings first lived on the shores of oceans and on the rivers, and then through infrastructure opened the landlocked areas of the planet. And today I can add—in the spirit of Krafft Ehricke—that the New Silk Road, now becoming the World Land-Bridge, will complete that phase of evolution by opening up all landlocked areas of the world.

Ehricke also said that joint international space research and travel *is* the next necessary phase of the evolution of mankind in the Universe, that mankind will become a space-based species.

Genius and Goodness in Our Future

So, I think we should be fully conscious that in this present crisis lies a tremendous opportunity to reach a new Renaissance, as significant and maybe even more significant than the change from the Middle Ages to the modern era; that if we break with the axioms of globalization, of deductive thinking, of all the things that have led to this crisis, and focus on the creativity of mankind as that which distinguishes us from other species, we can live to see—many of us can probably live to see—a world in which each child is educated universally and the normal condition of mankind is genius!

By fully developing that which is human—all of the potentials of the human species, as creative composers, scientists, engineers, extraordinary people discovering answers to questions that we haven't asked yet, like China going to the far side of the Moon—we will under-stand secrets of the Universe which we haven't yet imagined.

And we will become better people. I believe that the true nature of human beings is good, that every human being has a capacity for limitless self-perfection and goodness of the soul. And to accomplish that is within reach. And let's work for it.

CHAS FREEMAN

Things Fall Apart: America, Europe, and Asia in the New World Disorder

Ambassador Chas W. Freeman, Jr. (USFS, ret.), is a Senior Fellow at the Watson Institute for International and Public Affairs, Brown University. Ambassador Freeman was the U.S. ambassador to Saudi Arabia and the chief interpreter for President Richard Nixon during his 1972 trip to China.

We have entered a world in which, as William Butler Yeats put it in 1919:

> Things fall apart; the center
> cannot hold;
> Mere anarchy is loosed upon the world.

In Europe, in America, and in parts of Asia there is a sense of foreboding—an elemental unease about what is to come. There is vexing drift amidst political paralysis. Demagoguery is ascendant and the stench of fascism is in the air.

Developments in American politics are particularly discomfiting. The American people are belatedly beginning a discussion about the role of the United States in the world. We Americans should have had this conversation twenty-five years ago, when the Soviet Union collapsed and the Cold War ended. Now we are airing differences about foreign policy in circumstances of dispiriting international political and economic uncertainties. Few can even remember the optimism that prevailed when Germany reunited, Europe became whole and free, China joined the capitalist world, and Russia aspired to democratize and do the same.

Almost no one now sees much to admire in the results of U.S. foreign policy since these events. A few assert that our uses of force should have been more vigorous and sustained but most believe that recent U.S. military interventions have been counterproductive. A growing number of Americans express skepticism about interventions abroad.

In a world of ambiguities, the choice posed is binary. Are you for or against the exercise of U.S. military power? But the divisions between the sides have yet to be clearly drawn. The debate is ramping up as part of an election campaign driven by domestic malcontent, to which foreign policy is at most tangential. The discussion about America's international purposes and responsibilities is just beginning. It remains incoherent and as perplexing to Americans as it is alarming to allies, partners, and friends overseas.

Americans are having trouble formulating alternative approaches to foreign affairs, but they clearly reject more of the same. They may differ in their views of what "more of the same" means. But whatever it is, most don't want it. In this regard, Europeans do not seem much different.

Everyone is aware that major shifts in the distribution of global wealth and power are taking place. Ubiquitous malaise accounts for the welcome that many in both Europe and America have given to empty slogans masquerading as new ideas about how to manage borders, immigrants, foreign trade and investment, relations with allies and adversaries, and innovations in the existing international order. Further uncertainty arises from economic doldrums born of political gridlock, legislative defaults on fiscal policy, radical but unproductive monetary policies, the spread of authoritarianism, renewed antipathy between the West and Russia, and a lot of trash talk by the politically ambitious but intellectually challenged in both America and Europe.

The crumbling of the Pax Americana is an important contributor to the new world disorder. It is unnerving to Americans as well as to the allies and partners of the United States overseas. The best that might be said of it is that it also confuses America's adversaries. But, then, there is no agreement on who these adversaries are, still less what they may want.

With the disappearance of messianic totalitarianism, Americans succumbed to enemy deprivation syndrome. That is the queasy feeling of disorientation one has when one's military-industrial establishment no longer has an obvious, credible enemy on which to focus. European statecraft has traditionally accepted that allies on some matters can be adversaries on others, that military power is not in itself an answer to many problems, that long-term interests may require short-term sacrifice, and that it is often wiser to conciliate than to confront those seeking limited changes in the existing order. But these are novel thoughts for Americans schooled in international relations by the Cold War, when diplomacy resembled trench rather than maneuver warfare.

In many respects, the long contest with the Soviet Union turned America into a strategic "one-trick pony." Washington learned to resort to military deterrence and punishment through sanctions before considering diplomacy to eliminate the sources of discord that create the dangers it seeks to forefend. And deterrence is problematic, not only because it risks war by accident and doesn't always work, but because it immobilizes and defers potential conflicts rather than addressing their causes. Deterrence prevents immediate strife, buying time for diplomacy. But if there is no diplomacy, deterrence just stores up trouble for later, when the odds may shift to the advantage of one or the other side. This is especially likely when balances of power are rapidly shifting, as they are in the Indo-Pacific.

Americans now seem to be groping our way toward the realization that resolving the underlying issues driving contending sides toward combat may be a better approach to sustaining peace than trying to manage risk by promising to respond in kind to the use of force. If so, this is a healthy evolution that all should welcome. It offers renewed opportunities for U.S. allies and partners to leverage America's still enormous power to shape, steer, and maintain a better future than might otherwise evolve from the current global disorder.

But from an American perspective, Washington's European allies seem more muddled than ever. Europeans speak in many tongues and in contradictory ways. Britain's vote in favor of Brexit has just exacerbated Europe's confusion. Brexit promises to shatter the postwar order in Europe, to remove the British as intermediaries between the United States and "the Continent," and to deal a potentially fatal blow to Britain's special relationships with both. All this, as ill-considered proposals to renegotiate U.S. trans-Atlantic and trans-Pacific alliances, the global trade regime, and U.S.-Russia and U.S.-China relations ring out on the campaign trail in the United States.

A growing number of Americans understand that, if the United States does not heed the voices of its allies, it will in time cease to have any. But others ask how countries that spend relatively little on their own defense, preferring to leave it to Uncle Sam, can qualify as "allies" and equals rather than "protectorates." "Allies" are countries with mutual obligations and responsibilities to each other, not a one-sided dependency. Loose usage of the term "ally" conceals the fact that in Asia and the Middle East, the United States has wards and client states that it has taken under its unilateral protection, not "allies" committed to the common defense.

By contrast, the United States has always sought such allies in Europe, not satrapies or straphangers, still less servile sycophants. That is why Americans have been so supportive of the "European project." As the effort to unify Europe falters, so does American hope that Europe can avoid a return to the imbalances of power and politico-economic breakdowns that, on three occasions in the last century, required the United States to rescue and, finally, to garrison it.

To be frank, in present circumstances, to continue to be seen as allies and to be listened to as such by Americans, Europeans must alter their expectations of both themselves and America. They must do more in their own defense and form and communicate coherent views of what they need and don't need from the United States to supplement their own military power. They must equip themselves to persuade the American people that it's in the interest of the United States for them to get what they want. (The same is true of non-European partners like Japan and South Korea.) For better or ill, the world has entered an era of transactional relationships, not coalitions based on confrontation with a common global enemy, or mutual commitments to shared strategic interests and visions.

The call to rejustify, and at the same time restructure, America's overseas defense guarantees is a reminder that, for 160 years, the United States carefully avoided "entangling alliances." This stance ended only in 1949, when the United States joined Canada and ten European nations in forming NATO. Washington then sought to counter the perceived threat that Stalin's U.S.S.R. might seek to dominate—if not conquer—not just Europe, but the world beyond the Western Hemisphere, aggregating power in the Old World to the point that it could pose an existential challenge to the New. But the Soviet Union is no more. Notwithstanding today's efforts to portray Russia as implacably predatory, Europe faces no external menace comparable to those of yesteryear.

With American help, Europe recovered from World War II and strengthened its democratic political culture. It has enjoyed a quarter-century of peace, prosperity, and expansion of the rule of law since the Cold War ended. Europe may be much less than the sum of its parts, but it is not weak. European NATO members alone have a population more than four times that of Russia and a GDP that is nine times larger. They fall short of NATO's military budget targets but still spend at least three times more on defense as Russia. Some maintain formidably effective armed forces. There is no present requirement for Europeans to continue to rely mainly on U.S. forces for their defense. In these circumstances, it is hardly surprising that a growing number of Americans believe that the trans-Atlantic alliance is overdue for rebalancing.

Some ask, "if NATO is still the answer, what were the questions?" But, far from seeking to separate themselves from Europe, most Americans want a more equal security relationship with it. This is because three wars in the twentieth century (two hot and one cold) have shown that:

• Europe and America belong to a single geopolitical zone in which the security and well-being of each is inextricably connected to the other;

• A Europe-wide security architecture is needed to sustain security cooperation and keep peace among Europeans;

• America needs a link to that architecture to safeguard its vital interests in stability in Europe and Eurasia; and

• Europe requires American participation in its security architecture to preclude domination by its greatest power, Germany, and to enable it to balance and coexist peacefully with Russia.

These realities create an inescapable framework for trans-Atlantic cooperation, but they are not self-executing. They are undermined by Brexit and similar fissiparous tendencies elsewhere in Europe. They do not lead automatically to cooperative security, cooperative relationships with Russia or Turkey, or cooperative stabilization of the borderlands between Eurasia and Europe. The crafting of such arrangements demands statecraft that has been conspicuous by its absence since the end of the Cold War.

Peace and stability in Europe and Eurasia require recognition by Europe and Russia that both have a vital interest in a broadly united, prosperous, independent Ukraine. Such a Ukraine cannot emerge without restraint and reassurance by both. A model for this is the Austrian State Treaty of 1955, which established Austria as a sovereign, democratic state with safeguards for ethnic minorities. Austria cemented its freedom by declaring its permanent neutrality between East and West and developing a credible federal defense force. If this could be done for Austria at the height of the Cold War, it can be done for Ukraine in today's far less confrontational circumstances.

It would be in the interest of all, especially Ukrainians, to establish Ukraine as both a buffer and a bridge between Europe and Russia. Europeans and Russians have now proved beyond a reasonable doubt that each is prepared to frustrate and punish attempts by the other to absorb or dominate Ukraine. The United States has shown that it can be counted upon to back Europe militarily in resisting Russian intervention in Ukraine. The result is a dangerous impasse but also an opportunity. The two sides have exhausted coercive measures. Neither can hope to gain anything substantial from continuing competition for dominance in Ukraine. Escalating confrontation between NATO and Russia is costly and risky. It leads nowhere either side wishes to go. The negotiation of mutual guarantees of Ukraine's independence and neutrality on the model of Austria is the best remaining option.

But without a shared vision between Europe and Russia to frame such an outcome, the impasse will persist. This is an instance where a grand bargain is appropriate. The mutual pullbacks and reforms stipulated in the Minsk accords provide a potential starting point for a diplomatic process to consolidate the future place of an independent Ukraine between Europe and Russia. As at Minsk, Europe, not America, is best qualified to conceptualize and lead such a process, which needs to be part of a larger vision of cooperative security in Europe.

Wise American statecraft would welcome, not resist, Russian participation in the governance of affairs in both Europe and the Eurasian landmass as a whole. There are many existing institutional frameworks for this, including the OSCE, the NATO-Russia Council, the Council of Europe, the Shanghai Cooperation Council, and others. The reintegration of post-revolutionary France in the Concert of Europe after the Napoleonic wars showed how the inclusion of former adversaries in decision-making can promote long-term peace and stability in Europe. The exclusion of post-Wilhelmine Germany and post-Czarist Russia from the councils of Europe after World War I did not work out so well. That experience should drive home the peril of excluding great powers from an appropriate role in managing affairs in which they have a legitimate interest.

The United States, Europe, and Russia must also all adjust to a world in which China and India join Japan as Asian nations with global reach. This is a particularly difficult adjustment for the United States. America has dominated the Western Pacific for seventy-one years. It has become accustomed to being the custodian of the global commons and the indispensable arbiter of disputes in the region. Now it must accommodate a rising China, a more assertive India, and a more independent Japan.

Existing institutions, like ASEAN, are divided and ineffective in managing these issues. The shifting balances of power in the Asia-Pacific are mostly driven by economics. By contrast, the so-called U.S. "rebalance to Asia" is almost entirely military. The United States, Japan, and China are shouting past each other. But a piecemeal process of accommodation is unfolding amidst much histrionics about maritime territorial issues to which the United States is not a party.

The huge asymmetries between what is at stake in these issues for China and the United States are dangerous. To paraphrase Bismarck's prescient comments about the Balkans 26 years before World War I, all the rocks, reefs, and sandbars there are not worth the life of a single U.S. Marine. But if there is ever another war in Asia, it will come out of some damned silly thing in the South or East China Sea. Wars can happen even when they make no sense. In Asia, as in Europe, there is an urgent need for diplomacy as a substitute for military approaches that solve nothing, but risk much.

With the United States pushing back against Russia in the West and China in the East, the two are being nudged together. To counter Sino-Russian partnership, Japan is courting Russia, though not very effectively. China is reaching out to Europe. And China, Europe, Japan, Russia, and the United States are all courting India, which is playing hard to get. We have entered a world of many competing power centers and regional balances in which long-term vision and short-term diplomatic agility are at a premium. With the exception of India, none of the great powers at present displays both qualities.

This is the global context in which China has proposed to integrate the entire Eurasian landmass with a network of roads, railroads, pipelines, telecommunications links, ports, airports, and industrial development zones. If China's "One Belt, One Road" concept is realized, it will open a vast area to economic and intercultural exchange, reducing barriers to international cooperation in a 65-country zone with 70 percent of the world's population, with over 40 percent of its GDP, generating well over half of its current economic growth. The estimated cost of projects already on the drawing boards is at least eleven times what was spent on the Marshall Plan.

These massive infrastructure projects promise to deliver major increases in the speed of transport and telecommunications, to lower costs, and to create a great many new jobs. They will integrate Russia and Central Asia with both China and Europe, while connecting South Asia by land as well as by sea to the markets and natural resources of the countries to its north as well as to Africa.. By making land transport vastly more efficient and linking it to new ports and airports, the "One Belt, One Road" program will alter the balance between land and sea power, including in the Arctic regions now becoming accessible as a result of climate change.

In concept, the Belt and Road program is the largest set of engineering projects ever undertaken by humankind. Its potential to transform global geoeconomics and politics is proportional to its scale. It will create a greater arena for peaceful cooperation and competition than any empire ever did, and it will do so without military conquest or the use of force. It thereby offers an antidote to the strategic myopia, militarism, and financial gamesmanship that drive the new world disorder. It is an alternative to "more of the same" that the world should welcome and embrace.

VLADIMIR YAKUNIN

The Enormous Potential of a New Paradigm for All Mankind

Mrs. Zepp-LaRouche informed the conference that Dr. Vladimir Yakunin of Russia, chairman of the World Public Forum "Dialogue of Civilizations," was prevented from attending this panel and the conference due to diplomatic necessities in Russia at this moment.

ALAIN CORVEZ

Will American Hubris End by Choice, or in a Universal Combustion?

Col. (ret.) Alain Corvez is an international consultant and a former adviser to the French defense and interior ministries. He titled his address, "Will the American Hubris Come to an End, or Will It Disappear with Us in a Universal Combustion?"

Col. Corvez denounced the buildup of weapons in the heart of Europe by NATO, and in the Russian responses to it—that can extinguish not just the Europeans but all of mankind. NATO claims it is defensive, but it is offensive at the same time. It presents Russia as an imperial power and enemy, which is a falsehood so great, one wonders how the Europeans could ever take it seriously. The AEGIS system that the United States is deploying in Europe is capable of launching a nuclear attack anywhere on this planet.

It is unfortunate that France, which was critical of NATO under de Gaulle, joined the Alliance again under President Nicolas Sarkozy. Russia will not accept being crushed without responding with weapons that will not only mean World War III, but will extinguish mankind as a whole. American imperial hysteria must end before that happens.

As a French patriot, Corvez said, he must call on France to leave NATO. The alternative to the imperial hubris of the United States is the Chinese policy, which has proven that it is not imperialist but opts for cooperation. Europe must also abandon the technocratic Brussels EU and return to the concept of de Gaulle for a Europe of the sovereign nations.

Corvez concluded with a quote from a speech given by "a great French philosopher who also was an extraordinary statesman—General de Gaulle," in Mexico in 1964: There, de Gaulle warned against a "monstrous self-destruction" of humanity, but voicing confidence that "the fact that will dominate the future is the unity of our universe: one cause, that of man; one necessity, that of world progress; one duty, that of peace."

ULRICH SCHOLZ

War—A Pathology of the West

Lt. Col. (ret.) Ulrich Scholz of Germany is a former fighter pilot, NATO planner, and lecturer on air warfare.

War, said Col. Scholz, must be entirely eliminated as a means of politics. Clausewitz reached that conclusion long ago from his study of the Napoleonic Wars, but it is a lesson still not learned today. Politics must do without war, must eliminate war.

Continued on next page

No military action is acceptable that kills tens of children for the sake of eliminating a single terrorist. The "body counts" that have dominated in Western military approaches since the Vietnam War must end. We are violating our own ethics. We are making our actions not only useless, but actually criminal.

Our paradigms must change, which requires a cultural change—a learning process on a broad scale—in which media, politicians, and soldiers speak out against war on principled grounds. The well-being of Mankind must be the new principle—finally—after 150 million deaths caused by the wars of the past 200 years.

PANEL I
Question and Answer Session

The Q&A session, on June 25, began with a comment on Panel I by Lyndon LaRouche. This is an edited transcript.

Lyndon LaRouche: The important thing here is, what is the thing that is most important? It's mankind; the life and accomplishments of mankind. That's the issue. People die; it's regrettable, but the thing that is really regrettable is the loss of a creative life, or a process of creativity in life.

So, the problem is, that people think in terms of how to measure economy. Well, you really can't; economy cannot really be measured as such. There has to be a vehicle which has a reciprocal relationship to

Helga Zepp-LaRouche and Lyndon H. LaRouche, Jr.

the process as a whole. In the case now, what we're dealing with is that mankind appears to be running out of mankind's ability to produce; mankind's ability to maintain human life. All these things are there; and these are the kinds of thing for which we should be considered responsible. But the other thing is, how do we do something like that? How do we go into a field like building something, more productivity, and so forth? How do we do that? Well, you do that by discovering what man does in the process of being productive. If

man is being productive, how does man become productive? By creating conditions of life for mankind which are possible to achieve.

Now this means that we are responsible essentially for what is going to happen to humanity. And we are running out of opportunity for continuing man's life under those conditions. Therefore, we have to understand what we have to do in order to control man's needs; and it's not man's needs. The product is what man needs, but the cause is not that. The point is that in order for mankind to develop powers of scientific creativity per capita, per unit of operation,— how do we do that? We have to apply what we call real science; we have to put the emphasis on science, and increase the scientific concentration which the individual can contribute through different kinds of technologies.

This is a crucial issue; look at what we've lost so far. The United States, for example; the United States is made up of idiots. Why call them idiots? Because they don't take any account of the things that have to be done in order to create greater creativity useful for mankind per capita; it just doesn't exist for them. [applause] So therefore, the question is, mankind must change mankind! Mankind must understand how to change mankind's behavior! How do you create increased power of creativity? How do you improve all these powers? This is something which is not done; this is what, in general in the history now, is not done. We do not provide for the increment of the creative powers of mankind to create. To create what? To create the achievement of mankind; and that's what our chief failure has been.

How do we actually solve this problem? What you do is, you can go out and do some science. You apply science to create a method of creativity. Therefore, you base the whole thing not on mankind as such; you base it on the power of creativity. And that's what my responsibility is; that's what I do in the main. What I've done in general through most of my life, is that. You've got to increase the productive power of labor of the human mind. You have to give the individual human being a greater power of creative means for human life. That is where we fail. People talk about how *this* is going to be good, *that* is going to be good; that doesn't tell you anything. How do you develop the solar systems of the Universe? How do you do these things? You have to create something which is extremely creative for man's benefit, and this is essentially [inaudible].

First of all, we're looking at this issue of man as such. Man's ability to create higher levels of development of the human powers of mankind. The next thing is, how do we find things that are going to make mankind more successfully existent? And that's another question; and all these things are simple scientific questions. What we depend upon is driving what we call physical science, and driving it per capita to a higher level, always. Then in that process, you have to define what the means is by which you're going to do this. That's the point. And we have an *ignorantia* operation in society, mostly today. Most people who are called scientists are ignorant. Why? Because they limit themselves to certain categories which they are proved on; and these categories are worse than worthless. What mankind has to go out and create is a new creativity, and bring that increase of creativity into power. And this is what mankind does not do; it doesn't do it in the United States, except for a few people. It doesn't do it in other parts of the world. It goes through a performance, and in general in the past century, this policy of management of man's development has been a failure—a profound failure. Mankind's condition of life, mankind's ability to protect life, has been a failure. The behavior of mankind has been a failure.

This is the point: When we develop new kinds of technologies which increase mankind's powers and ability to create, to make new discoveries, to advance,— these are the things on which mankind depends. For example, we go out into the Universe to find solutions for what are called scientific problems. That is a technology; so, it's the increase of the technologies in all senses of technologies. These are the things on which mankind's continued existence depends. You can't just use something; you can not just adopt something. You have to actually make discoveries, as I have done in much of my own work. You create a new technology which was not known before, enhance that technology, and apply it.

My concern is always to come up with a new technology—a more advanced technology, one which overturns and obviates the need for an existing technology. Without that ability to see the future of mankind, to see new technologies,— For example, what do you use? We use water in a galactic way; that's a very important technology. I would say, just to keep this as short as possible, my specialty is concentrating on the revolution in the applicable technologies; and that is the only device by which I know that mankind can improve the requirements for mankind now.

Helga Zepp-LaRouche: Now we have an open floor for discussion. You are welcome to address anyone on this panel on issues which were raised.

Leona Meyer-Kasai: I have one question for Mr. LaRouche. You have emphasized a lot the Manhattan

Partial view of attendees at the conference.

Project and the music work, singing in the chorus. And the question is, we have the danger of World War III, and you emphasize now that we need to have now advancement in science. How does it go together with the chorus work? Maybe you can elaborate what it does for mankind?

LaRouche: I think first of all, you have to go to a corrected approach to the question as such. Mankind has to create creativities; that's the function. Mankind, as a scientist, must create new creativities which are not just forms, but are actually revolutionary physical changes, physical improvements in what mankind can do; and the ability to develop that. The average citizen in society has no idea of what science is; that's the real difficulty in trying to deal with this problem. They don't know what science is, they have no concept of what science is. You will find that most Russians will do that; you will find that the China population is developing these powers very strongly. China is progressing at a very high rate of development; beyond the attention of most people. It's a difficult problem to solve and to manage, but it works. So, the question is essentially, mankind has to discover what the means are by which mankind can make a change in the way the individual

thinks, which brings an improvement in the development of the human situation.

Yada Molla: Hello. I would like to thank you very much for the first session; it was really interesting. My name is Yada Molla [as heard], and I am from Syria. I am here in Berlin doing my PhD in international relations and cultural diplomacy and trying to figure out the cultural heritage for bringing peace and reconciliation in post-conflict Syria. My question is actually on the link between all the presentations that we had, and the last speech from Mr. LaRouche. Because as a Syrian, yes we were kind of on the right track towards a real development; maybe small steps towards democracy. And we were looking at creativity, we were looking at the potential of cultural heritage in engaging with the society, engaging with the people. We were trying to work on really shaping our identity in a modern way, although with a strong basis in our heritage, the heritage that gave us values to live together all those years since the 10,000 years before crisis.

And there were a lot of other projects that have been done by civil society in terms of discovery centers for children, to bring science into the main ideas of the children and to bring it in the basis of their thinking and development. But, how can we, in a way with another — OK, now [war] is happening in Syria, but next we don't know where it's going to happen. How can we stop the interruption of such a development? There are nations which have a destiny; a destiny to not develop, a destiny not to go into democracy and not to go into real life simply because there are other agendas that are already set for such regions. And that's the most suitable solution for such countries,— the chaos. Syria was with zero debt, with a very good agenda towards engaging cultural heritage and creativity and science. There was a big change happening in the last ten years before the crisis, so in the last 15 years onwards, until the boom of Syria in 2009-2010. And then all of a sudden, everything has collapsed. Of course, there are problems in Syrian society that maybe we have to raise our voices for; but the main big problem was more of an influence of geopolitical interests. So, my question is, how can we really make the balance? Yes, we need to create things for our future, we need to create diversity, we need to create creativity plus infrastructure, or a possibility to build that. But how can we stop that interruption?

LaRouche: What I would recommend is to turn attention to the question of science as such; and I would talk about what has been done by [inaudible]. The point is that the idea of science—mental science and so forth—is little understood. It's known in history, but it's very poorly represented, and therefore, people are given so-called "practical" kinds of methods of science. And these practical methods of science are not competent. The question is, can we find a characteristic in terms of any kind of function? Can we find a characteristic which is typical of mankind? Let's take something in space. Yes, we can. And what we should do, essentially, is take these kinds of things which we can explain in that way practically; and that will work. The issue is when you don't have the right kind of advice in terms of how to go at this thing and express it.

Chas Freeman: Can I offer a different answer? Respect for international law would be a good place to start. Syria is a sovereign nation; and foreign countries have no right to intervene, either directly or indirectly, in its internal affairs. I happened to be in Damascus at the end of March, beginning of April 2011, when the unrest in the Southwest began; and I therefore can say that there were grave miscalculations on all sides. On the part of Bashar Assad and his government, there was the misjudgment that if Hosni Mubarak in Egypt, or Zine Ali in Tunisia could be easily overthrown, if Yemen could be cast into anarchy, that this could also happen to him. And that therefore, he had to act to pre-empt and prevent an unravelling of his own regime; and he over-reacted. Outside forces—the Saudis, the Israelis, the Qataris, the Americans, the Turks—made the equal and opposite miscalculation, that with a little push, the regime could change. All of these judgments were incorrect, and almost 400,000 dead Syrians later, with 11 million Syrians displaced from their homes, with 5 million Syrian children not receiving education, the war continues. And some of Syria's neighbors find the continuation of war more convenient than peace. But if we return to the principle of international law, and allow Syrians to settle their own problems, we would all be better off; that's my answer.

Question: Hello. I have a question for actually everyone. We talked recently about exiting NATO, but that's not enough. I would very much like to hear thoughts on the question of a new security order for the entire world, so that we get out of this entire NATO dynamic. We completely overhaul,— Just as we've been discussing for economics, the economic system is bankrupt, we need an overhaul. The BRICS have started; China has initiated the Silk Road policy. So, what would that be like for security? I think that's the next step.

Zepp-LaRouche: Well, I'm a strong proponent for a completely new international security architecture. Mankind has reached the point where, if we don't stop thinking in terms of blocs, we will not make it. Geopolitics must be completely banned from our thinking—and therefore I have a slightly different opinion than what was expressed by Chas—that we must move into a new domain where joint economic interests will be provided for by the World Land-Bridge. Where all continents work for the common good in a global development partnership, and therefore they have a common interest; and therefore you can have a joint international security architecture, which would be basically taking into account all the security interests of everybody. I think this is absolutely Possible. Nuclear disarmament would be one big step; but also other weapons of mass destruction would fall under that.

And in a certain sense, if we do not accomplish a world without war, and I fully agree with Mr. Scholz that war in times of thermonuclear weapons cannot be a means of solving conflict; or we don't exist. And that has to become a public debate; because if you don't move in this way, I don't think that you can construct any kind of regional security arrangement—trans-Atlantic, Pacific, whatever—without this thing going awfully wrong. We should have the alarm bells really ringing as loudly as possible; we are close to annihilation. If it goes wrong, we don't exist. During the time of Kennedy, people were aware of it; the Cuban Missile Crisis was understood. Kennedy said, if it comes to the use of thermonuclear weapons, the people who will be dead in the first hours will be happy compared to those who die a few weeks later. And that condition has not changed.

I think we have to have a complete revolution in thinking, with the idea of a win-win cooperation taking into account the interest of the other, which was one of the basic ideas of the Peace of Westphalia in 1648, ending the Thirty Years' War. You can solve the problem, but how do you accomplish that in practice? How do you solve the problem of Israel, of Iran, of Pakistan? All these things are powder kegs, and therefore you need a global approach where the big powers—the United States, Russia, China, India, and others—are working together. If we don't get that, we will be dead; that is my firmest conviction.

Col. Ulrich Scholz: I think the United Nations is the only international organization we have, and we shouldn't just try to re-invent one; we should just make it effective. Which includes, for example, America accepting the International Criminal Court and international law for everybody. The Security Council should really be empowered to take care of peace in this world.

On NATO's part, I'd like to put a little warning out when it comes to dismantling the organization. From my technical experience with NATO across the nations, when you send NATO troops somewhere, they are standardized; they know how to work together. And this has developed over decades, so there is a treasure, really. If you send them somewhere, they know how to do things. What I would take away from NATO is the strategic ability to wage war, and I would open NATO up as a security system. I would introduce that Russia comes in there; that we have a military arm for the United Na-

tions which is capable. So I think this is for me the most practical step if we want to contain all these fires spreading in the world, come to a better understanding of each other, and solve problems peacefully. If we are all in the same system, we can work together and be more effective.

Col. Alain Corvez: [translated from French] I agree with what Col. Scholz just said, and I also agree with what Chas Freeman said in response to these two young women. I think—concerning the question of the Syrian young lady—that there are countries for which the great ideas are very far from their own preoccupations; they want a world where everybody will cooperate, but those populations are actually under the bombs. And I don't think it helps to give priority to great ideas which cannot be realized. Of course, humanity has to cooperate with all the populations on this planet to eliminate war; but man is man, and it's not by a kind of order that man is transformed into an angel. I want to approve what Chas Freeman said and what Col. Scholz said. We have an organization which is theoretically in charge of having law respected by all nations without going to war. So, we have to recall the United Nations to its mission, and we have to use this organization which still exists today.

But to propose that people who are suffering the worst—I just came back from Syria,— great ideas are good, but what those people want first of all is a solution to their immediate problems. And as the ambassador said, we have to respect the right of people to dispose of themselves; and it is not up to the strongest to decide what will be done to the weaker.

Chas Freeman: I would like to say that, if you want to get to a world free of geopolitics, ironically the only country that has the luxury to do that is my own. Bismarck correctly described us as having meek Canadian neighbors to the north, fun-filled Mexican neighbors to the south, and on the east and west, neighbors who are fish. So, we have a geopolitical position which gives us the luxury to disengage; and for most of our history we did. And in some sense, the debate that is going on in the United States now is about that. We can to some extent disengage. The question is, is that wise?

I'd like to buttress the point that Col. Scholz made. I was the American ambassador in Riyadh during the Gulf War of 1990-91. What we discovered was that the 32 nations that participated in that war to liberate

Kuwait, were forced to use NATO methodology and doctrine in order to be able to work together on the battlefield. There was no alternative; it is the only set of software that produces interoperability between nations with different military traditions. So it is something valuable in that sense. But we must also remember that in the 20th Century, the United States disengaged twice from Europe, and then found itself compelled to be drawn back in. So I think we need to find a balance here; and that balance probably begins in my mind with Europe taking responsibility for its own affairs.

Most Americans, by the way, regard foreign policy as a largely irrelevant annoyance. We don't have to have a foreign policy; we can afford not to have one. That is unique; but you better hope that we do have one that stresses cooperation with a European-led European order.

Ashraf Matar: Hello, first of all. My name is Ashraf Matar, and I am from Syria. I want to express first that I am happy that you exist, and this institute exists. I never heard of it until one year ago, and thanks to Toby and the branch of the institute in Essen, I knew about you and about this conference. I have many questions and many points to clear with Col. Scholz first. You defined three factors for any war, but I think we are missing the economic factor, which is the most important, and that's what's happening now in Syria. I was part of the revolution, and when the revolution started to be Islamic, I left and I was persecuted by both sides. We discovered then that this plan was set since 2005 and maybe before that.

And to Mr. Freeman, since you were the ambassador in Saudi Arabia, actually I wonder about this friendship between Saudi Arabia and the United States. You are friends with the people who are the most founding jihadists, founding terrorism. The second thing is that the interference in the nations, this is not something new. [applause] Even when you visited Syria, all of you, I doubt that any of you had an idea of what was happening about that before. Even in Iraq, the democracy and the freedom—they can feel it now I think, and in Syria also. And this program, or this plan which has been in Iraq, my mother read about it 10 years before it started, in 1981, exactly like it happened in 1991 when Iraq invaded Kuwait; and it was a surprise for everyone. So, please, if you have some answers, since you are responsible for many years.

Zepp-LaRouche: I have to ask you to be relatively concise, because we have to stop at one o'clock.

Scholz: About adding economics to the list of the causes of war, I have included economics in the political aims, because all politics, all wars are about economics in the end. So I don't want to make a differentiation there; war is just for me useless. It's the wrong way, and that was my argument—for any reason.

Freeman: I agree with Col. Scholz's analysis. I would add one other question to the three that he mentioned, or maybe two questions. One, before you start a war, ask, "And then what?" We don't ask; we use violence for its own sake. And finally, ask how you are going to make a peace at the end. What is your war termination strategy? If you don't have one, don't go to war.

With respect to Saudi Arabia, I will simply say that the U.S. relationship with Saudi Arabia has never been based on common values. It has been based on common interests. And until very recently, the Saudis did not pursue independent policies in the Middle East; they looked to the United States to tend their interests. They have no confidence in the United States now, and therefore, they are striking out on their own; and that is causing a lot of problems, I agree. Syria is very much a proxy war between many forces, including Saudi Arabia, Iran, Turkey, ourselves, the Israelis—who, by the way, say openly that they hope the war goes on forever, because it serves their interests for Syria to be in a state of anarchy. So there are many people responsible for the tragedy in Syria, not just some Syrians. Many foreigners as well.

Zepp-LaRouche: I would like to add that the truth about September 11, which is now about to come out in the U.S. Congress, will shed light on the true character of the wrong people in the United States and the Saudi regime. And that has to be cleared up, because if you don't get to the root of that, there will be no end to the financing of jihad, of ISIS, al-Qaeda, and similar organizations. But the good news is that in the United States Congress, the new law will be debated, and in all likelihood the 28 pages will be released and published. Not only that, but also the 80,000 pages suppressed by the FBI about the Florida component of the planning for September 11. I think without such a catharsis, cleaning up the roots of what happened in the last 15 years, I don't think this thing can be resolved. But the news gives reason for optimism that this can be done.

The Crisis of the Trans-Atlantic Financial System and How to Overcome It

JACQUES CHEMINADE

Lyndon LaRouche's Method of Physical Economy

Jacques Cheminade, a presidential candidate in France, gave the keynote address for Panel II.

The trans-Atlantic financial system in which we are living—based on appropriating money—leads to chaos or war, or more precisely and more tragically, to a combination of both. The preceding speakers have shown that the current world is more dangerous than it ever was at the height of the Cold War. The system, by its very nature, is criminal. Justice has become a cash-convertible commodity while fraudsters operate in packs, committing frauds with systemic effects which have turned our stock markets into gigantic crime scenes.

Too big to fail, too big to manage, too big to jail: an industry of unpunished corruption has become the norm and the heads of our central banks have become counterfeiters. The mere fines that financial criminals are hit with give them in effect the right to perpetuate their fraud and trafficking, while the fines are paid with the bank's reserves, to the detriment of employees, depositors and even shareholders.

Today, these megabanks bluntly admit, as JPMorgan Chase did in its analysis published on May 28, 2013, "The Euro Area Adjustment: About Halfway There": their intention is to dissolve democratic systems in order to enforce increasingly ferocious austerity measures on people.

Lyndon LaRouche's forecast, made back in the 1970s, of would happen, is now being echoed, after it did happen, by all those who are preoccupied with the future of mankind, as the criminals operate in broad daylight while fictitious capital comprised of debts and financial securities is growing, at the expense of the creation of wealth in the real economy.

However, contrary to analysts that enjoy doom and gloom or practice selective indignation, LaRouche, from the start, reacted against this state of affairs by outlining alternative policies. He didn't just denounce policies that were becoming increasingly intolerable and leading to war by their inner logic of looting and seeking, once again, "Lebensraum" to the East, but he proposed one after the other win-win projects on a world scale: a "productive triangle" among Paris, Berlin and Vienna after the fall of the Berlin Wall, a "Eurasian landbridge," together with his wife Helga, a "new silk road," and a "world landbridge" for peace and mutual development. LaRouche, without hesitation, said "NO" and then defined another frontier.

LaRouche's Approach

When I first became aware of his ideas, over forty years ago, three things struck me immediately. First, the fact that his concept of economics was not derived from statistics and currencies, but from the creative powers of the human mind. As in Edgar Allen Poe's "Purloined Letter," this fact eludes us, although its reality is blinding. As the heir of the American revolutionary tradition and as a critical reader of Marx, LaRouche revolted against the Malthusian vision of the Club of Rome, the latter sharing with financial capitalism the method of linear extrapolation of existing resources, without taking into account those that the human mind is capable of discovering.

LaRouche is unique in that his initial reaction of rejection also contains the foundation of the required alternative. To criticize without proposing, he often argues, only leads to pessimism, or even worse to destructive violence. To criticize the dominant order without presenting an alternative only leads to hateful nihilism, which led to terrible ravages in the 20th Century or again today in Europe, which is becoming xenophobic and communitarianist.

LaRouche's approach is above deduction and induction; based on the unwavering determination to change the social environment to make it worthy of mankind, and to do so with what I call, in French, a universal empathy that leads him to always say aloud what he conceives. He defines himself and acts as a human being living in the future, and is inspired by those in the past, who have shown us the way out of dead ends by their capacity to discover realities beyond the egoistical sphere of sense perception—that is, by the quality of *agape* which distinguishes human beings from all other species known so far.

The second thing which struck me in his thinking is that he understood how "liberal" ideology has by definition no directionality, and therefore allows all transgressions. LaRouche immediately understood that the moral deregulation, produced by Woodstock and May 68, would lead one decade later to financial deregulation, and to the mutually assured greed that generates crime.

He also demonstrated the destructive consequences of the August 1971 decoupling of gold from the dollar, an agreement that offered the world like a chicken coop without protection to the foxes of finance, and of Margaret Thatcher's October 27 1986 "Big Bang," which opened the City of London to the wildest types of financial speculation by the entire world's financial entities.

Then, in 1999, LaRouche denounced the scrapping of Franklin Roosevelt's Glass-Steagall Act, because this was not a technical measure, but rather a licence to loot given to the major financial institutions in the jungle they had created in this way, which rendered entire nations impotent to defend their people.

At the same time, and this is a supplementary proof of his originality, LaRouche warned that unbridled economic liberalism, akin to the sort that went rampant during the 1930s, leads to fascist takeovers, as now openly admitted in JPMorgan Chase's report. I remember LaRouche telling us that economic liberals and financial libertarians are like drunkards: they fill themselves up with financial assets, have a hangover on the weekend and wake up as fascists on Monday morning. On December 2, 1971, during a debate with leading Keynesian economist Abba Lerner at Queen's College New York, LaRouche brought Lerner to say that if the world had supported the policies of Hjalmar Schacht, "Hitler would not have been necessary." Schacht was Hitler's Finance Minister; he was the "financial wizard" who organized his rise to power and imposed austerity and financial manipulations, with the full backing of the City and Wall Street.

In 1971, Lerner promoted this "liberal authoritarian" policy for the Brazilian military dictatorship, a policy adopted two years later by Pinochet and the Argentine generals, which led to their atrocities. Since then, since 1971, U.S. journalists have been ordered to stop mentioning LaRouche, and if ever they are obliged to do so, to slander him and pervert his message. This only comes as a surprise for those who have never consulted the United States and British press between 1930 and 1938.

In 1989, after a sham political trial, recognized as a total frame-up by those who looked into the matter, including by Gaullists of the French Resistance, LaRouche was sentenced to a long prison term. When he left that prison, he was even more determined to fight.

The Becoming

The third thing which struck me is LaRouche's capacity to see the world as one whole, in a permanent state of becoming. As an American patriot, he always sought, "as far as in China" as the Muslims would say, what other patriots have contributed to the world, while fighting for a dialogue of cultures and civilizations.

The creative capacities of human beings have their roots in the works of classical culture, "classical" in the sense that it attempts to awaken in each human being the best he or she has, to inspire his spirit of discovery, with art and science advancing at the same pace. Hence, the importance, as LaRouche stresses, of Einstein, who starts from what he calls a *Gedankenexperiment*, a thought experiment in the physical universe, which he nourished by his daily practice of playing the violin, in the company of Mozart and Beethoven.

On the opposite end stands Bertrand Russell, who starts from mathematical principles in a universe composed of axioms and postulates from which he derives subsequently, in the smallest possible number, the logical properties. Einstein said *"Although I am a typical loner in my daily life, my awareness of belonging to the invisible community of those who strive for truth, beauty, and justice prevents me from feelings of isolation."*

That same awareness is what always inspired LaRouche, who never become discouraged, even in prison, because of his personal commitment. This awareness also led him to fight Russell's ideology, a destructive stamp our society still bears, the ideology of an Empire managing the logic of a finite world that excludes progress and demands that *"the less prolific races will have to defend themselves against the more prolific by methods which are disgusting even if they are necessary."* (Russell, 1923).

Alan Yue

LaRouche (third from right) handily defeated leading Keynsian economist in a debate at Queens College, New York, Dec. 2, 1991.

Consider everything LaRouche is fighting against today, from the now criminal provocations of NATO to depopulation policies. We are faced with the implacable coherence of a culture of death and we must defeat its logic if the world is to have a future.

At the basis of evil, there is this conception of a finite world, created once and forever, and where the technology deployed by human beings does not serve to improve the living conditions for all, but to oppress them and, in the end, to destroy them.

Thus, LaRouche's method of physical economy should first and foremost be seen as in opposition to a universe that is "running down," incapable of producing the necessary resources to allow a world population the conditions for a future. So-called "realists" and "reasonable people," who follow the rules of the game of the system, in reality contribute to its collapse by the very fact that they operate within it without fighting it.

Now we have arrived at a point in history where a change of system, a just concept of economy and man are necessary for the survival of all. Money has no intrinsic value; it is only an instrument and only acquires value through what it promotes. So what is the goal to be reached? LaRouche stipulates that the goal of an economic policy worthy of the name is to create the most favorable conditions possible for the development of the creative powers of individuals, in a society that fosters that: health, education, R&D, etc. The key economic criterion is not to buy cheap and sell expensive or to acquire rare goods which others do not have, but to increase what LaRouche calls the relative potential population density of society, i.e., its carrying capacity made possible by the constant introduction of new technologies applying the discoveries of new physical principles. The late Russian scientist and space expert Pobisk Kuznetsov called this fundamental criterion the "La," La for LaRouche.

Hence, physical economy, in contrast to the monetarist economy which makes money a value in itself, aims to increase this transformational power as a function of the potential physical development of society, per capita, per surface unit and per household. The idea is not to "push to the limit" a given technology at a given time, since that produces a progressive decrease of energy, but to overcome that loss by the introduction of new modes of production. That means more "free energy" compared to the amount of energy used. Both in terms of energy and technology, the challenge is to increase the energy-flux density produced per capita, per unit surface and per gram of material used.

Past versus Future Economy

This defines, for example, the relative superiority of nuclear power over other modes of energy production, but also its inferiority, if one remains at the level of nuclear fission obtained from Pressured Water Reactors (PWRs) such as those designed by Westinghouse in the 1960s. Progress is defined by the transition to ever more productive modes of producing fission—fourth generation nuclear fission—and from there, to thermonuclear fusion. Thus, nuclear energy is not a technical method at a given moment, but a dynamic sustained and enhanced by human creation. The physical constraint that will force nuclear energy beyond the current methods is the challenge of space travel, which will require fusion power and probably, much later, matter/anti-matter reactions.

Are we daydreaming? No, because these things exist in a universe which is being constantly created, and because the increasing mastery of its principles can only be based on cooperation to achieve a common aim brining together the different components of humanity.

In short, that means peace through mutual economic development, not so much because of the goal to be reached, as because of the mobilization required to reach it and the quality of development of those who are part of it.

Lyndon LaRouche has always insisted on the quality of cooperative work needed to implement his method, although "method" is a word I don't like, and which in French is associated with the formal and even formalin. I prefer to speak of the "spirit of discovery," which makes economics the most beautiful of all sciences, since it demands constant discovery.

Just imagine children and adolescents rediscovering new physical principles and experimenting with them, as some of you have done. In this case, contrary to the Bertrand Russell method—and in this case it's definitely a method, just as Descartes' *Discourse on Method* is—the children do not learn and regurgitate formulas, but they discover, as little Einsteins, constructions in the physical economy. It is among these children and adolescents that physical economy, as envisioned by LaRouche, begins in service of that which is human in human beings.

What is the source that will nourish this economy? For LaRouche, this cannot come from financial returns or taxes, that are based on what already exists in monetary terms, but rather on the future creation of wealth made possible by productive credit.

While the Anglo-Dutch system defines itself, as we said, by the possession and the issue of money, and by the control over states by a financial oligarchy of central bankers, the "American System" of LaRouche is characterized by productive public credit, that is, by the power given to a country to issue credit for great projects aimed at increasing the potential relative population-density, and both the energy and the technology-flux density.

That was the conception of Alexander Hamilton, the founder of the American System of political economy, which is little known in Europe. Hamilton introduced Article 1, Section 8 into the U.S. Constitution, which gives power to the U.S. Congress to issue letters of credit on the Federal government in favor of the Public Treasury, which in turn calls on the National Bank to coordinate the allocation of these credits. This concept of public credit redefines the very nature of debt: It reflects the intention of the government to pursue an action it deems necessary and to incur debt to achieve it. There is a "debt" incurred, but with no money circulating in the process, as the credit- money is just the means by which state credit is transferred and is not "liquidity."

Hence, this system of public credit defines "value" as a means to increase the productive powers of labor (again, per capita, per unit of surface area, and per unit of materials employed). We have a physical economy

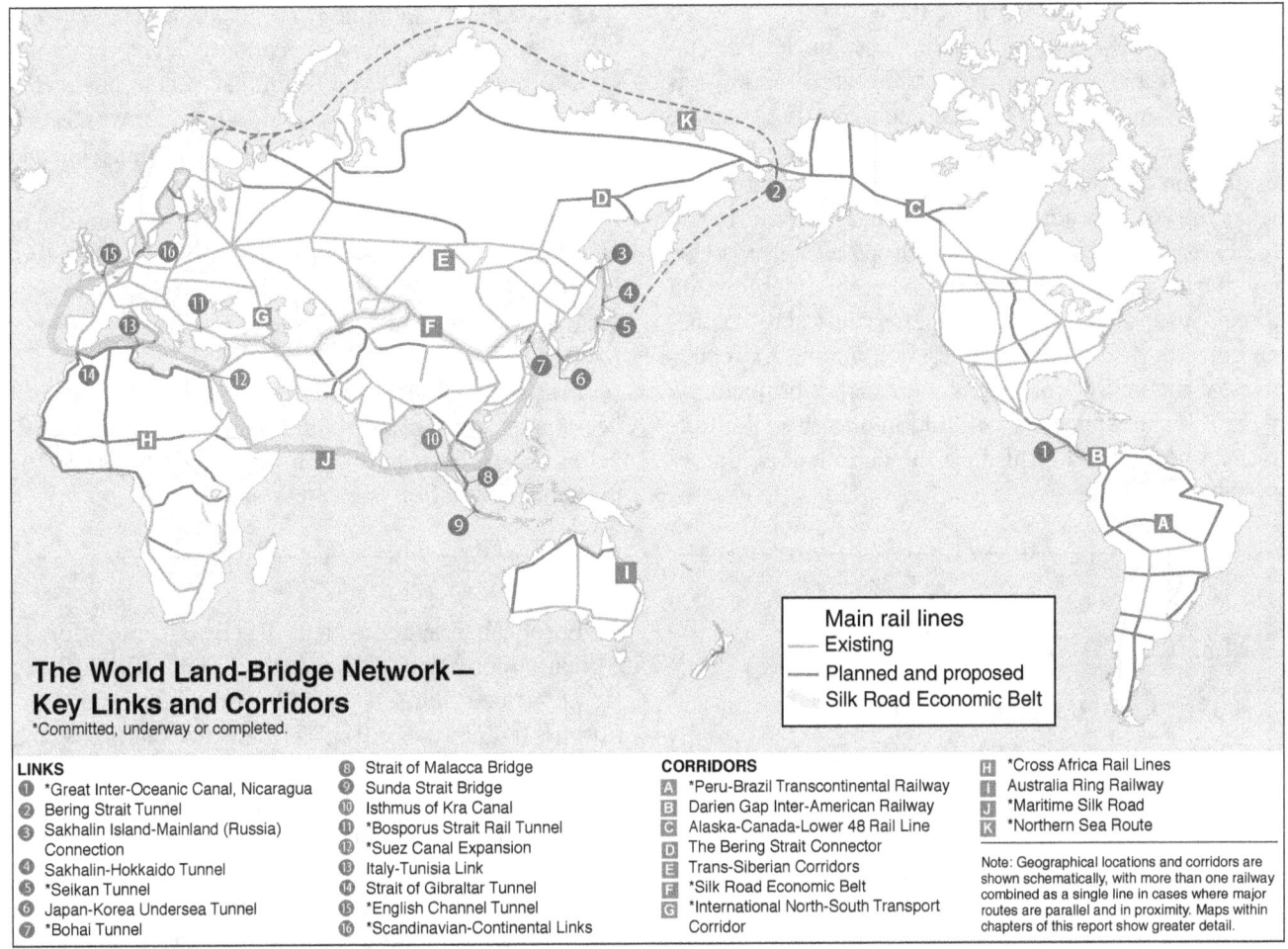

**The World Land-Bridge Network—
Key Links and Corridors**
*Committed, underway or completed.

Main rail lines
— Existing
— Planned and proposed
— Silk Road Economic Belt

LINKS
1. *Great Inter-Oceanic Canal, Nicaragua
2. Bering Strait Tunnel
3. Sakhalin Island-Mainland (Russia) Connection
4. Sakhalin-Hokkaido Tunnel
5. *Seikan Tunnel
6. Japan-Korea Undersea Tunnel
7. *Bohai Tunnel
8. Strait of Malacca Bridge
9. Sunda Strait Bridge
10. Isthmus of Kra Canal
11. *Bosporus Strait Rail Tunnel
12. *Suez Canal Expansion
13. Italy-Tunisia Link
14. Strait of Gibraltar Tunnel
15. *English Channel Tunnel
16. *Scandinavian-Continental Links

CORRIDORS
A. *Peru-Brazil Transcontinental Railway
B. Darien Gap Inter-American Railway
C. Alaska-Canada-Lower 48 Rail Line
D. The Bering Strait Connector
E. Trans-Siberian Corridors
F. *Silk Road Economic Belt
G. *International North-South Transport Corridor
H. *Cross Africa Rail Lines
I. Australia Ring Railway
J. *Maritime Silk Road
K. *Northern Sea Route

Note: Geographical locations and corridors are shown schematically, with more than one railway combined as a single line in cases where major routes are parallel and in proximity. Maps within chapters of this report show greater detail.

in the service of man, in which the physical production of tangible goods resulting from the income generated by the project itself will supply the means to pay back the debt. Money only has a value if it is linked to the issuance of credit. Therefore, it can be called an "antiusury" system.

Abraham Lincoln said, "Man is not the only animal who labors, but he is the only one who improves his workmanship." It is on such improvement, in contrast to monetary speculation or hopes of financial profit, that the entire Hamiltonian system is based, a system expanded and further developed by Lyndon LaRouche.

This approach is totally contrary to what has prevailed in the United States and Europe since the suppression of national banks and the public credit system. In the United States, it is by perverting the Constitution that the system was handed over to the megabanks and Wall Street. In Europe, it was the destructive development of the European Union which forced the nations to depend on credit from the same megabanks. The result is what we have defined at the beginning of this presentation: financial looting and a world, just as in the 1930s, headed straight toward war if nothing is done to stop it.

The World to Come

LaRouche's approach has been partly taken up in the agreement of the Eurasian Economic Union and the Chinese "One Belt, One Road" project of the New Silk Road, with their credit institutions, such as the BRICS New Development Bank which has recently doubled its capital and intends to sign contracts in the currencies of the member states rather than in dollars or in euros. Therein lies a hope, and not in our transatlantic world that is running into a wall.

Therefore, let us leave behind the world of before, and fight for the world to come. Let us imagine teams of scientists, engineers, qualified technicians and workers, combining their skills and know-how on the scale of Eurasia and the world, and given the resources needed to use and permanently expand them.

Imagine how they will spark a new spirit of co-development and win-win partnership, and Lyndon LaRouche's method of physical economy. Imagine the United States and us Europeans rediscovering our sense of mission and our constitutional principles. Is that not what the Ode to Joy, although it has become banal, really expresses? We must take Europe back from those counterfeiters of the European Union, in order to build a real Europe of projects and fatherlands and beyond, an entente, détente and cooperation among the countries of the entire world. It is with such a project, and what it inspires, that we will find in ourselves the self-respect needed to to finish off the dominant predatory system.

LaRouche's challenge is to muster in the 21st Century all means of a physical economy devoted to mankind to build peace through mutual development, exactly those means which were mobilized for war during a 20th Century which was financially imperial and ideologically Russellite.

Physical economy can become the most beautiful of all sciences since it will produce and transmit the good. It is the science of the human mind. LaRouche shows us the road to hope, which will not be made of roses but of combat.

Hence, such is our conviction, man can and must become the artist of the universe by exploring domains yet unknown to us but which we can master, since the principle of creation is innate in us.

MARCO ZANNI

The Collapse of the European Financial System and the Failure of the Banking Union

Marco Zanni, MEP for the Italian Five Star Movement (M5S), is the head of the M5S delegation in the Economic and Monetary Affairs Committee of the European Parliament. He has introduced several Glass-Steagall resolutions in the European Parliament and visited U.S. Congressmen to push for action on Glass-Steagall legislation.

Zanni opened by saying the Brexit vote was, for him, a "surprising result," sending a strong message of democracy to the EU. The EU has been imposing an integration "on a false basis," he said, referring to the European financial system. The Brexit vote offers a great opportunity to discuss the failure of the EU. He described himself as a "strong supporter of Europe, but not of the EU." The EU does not have a policy of growth, which must be restored—growth of the real economy, of small and medium-sized enterprises (SMEs), not of speculation, finance, or big banks.

He focussed on the Single Supervisory Mechanism (SSM), operating through the European Central Bank (ECB), as it exemplifies the problem he is addressing. The SSM, through its "stress tests," never looked at the exposure to financial debt, that is, derivatives, looking instead at "level 3 assets," the prices of which are determined by internal models, and therefore cannot be challenged. The SSM never looked at risk related to derivatives, which he said is the basis of its failure. Instead of determining how to invest in the real economy, the ECB tried to make the system "safer," by pushing more financialization, that is, to make it safer for the biggest banks. Securitization, he said, will not permit growth of the real economy.

Zanni concluded by proposing two steps: (1) a modern, European Glass-Steagall, which would allow banks to focus on the real economy; and (2) an Italian government takeover (as a model) of the Banca Monte dei Paschi di Siena, one of Italy's leading banks, to take it out of trading and derivatives, and instead, use it to invest in the real economy.

DAISUKE KOTEGAWA

Japan's Outlook Concerning Eurasian Cooperation

Daisuke Kotegawa is the research director of the Canon Institute for Global Studies, Japan, and former representative of Japan to the IMF.

Kotegawa spoke of his experience of more than 35 years in the Japanese Ministry of Finance. He spoke of what he learned from his hands-on involvement in liquidating large banks in the late 1990s, from which he concluded that investment banks are interested only in rich people and gambling.

In contrast, he spoke of the importance of the Abe-Putin meetings in Sochi last month. It had been expected that not much would happen, but he received a private report that the meetings went very well. Prime Minister Shinzo Abe is now expected to attend an economic forum in Vladivostock in September, and Putin will come to Japan later this year. This is the basis for optimism in Japan.

Japan, he said, is moving back into nuclear power generation. By 2030, there will be 24 new nuclear plants opened in Japan.

He spoke of the "new bubble" in Japan, the wave of Chinese tourists. When he was in the Finance Ministry, he was in charge of Japanese assistance to China. Approximately $10 billion a year was invested, for six years, in railroads, airports, ports, telephone networks, and fertilizer plants. As a result of the progress of the economy in China, reflected today in the Silk Road policy, 5 million Chinese visited Japan as tourists last year.

In conclusion, he returned to the problem of the financial system. Keeping equity in banks (as in Basel III and various European Central Bank schemes) won't stop gambling, but the gambling must be stopped. The focus, he said, must return to manufacturing and infrastructure.

LEONIDAS CHRYSANTHOPOULOS

Global Crisis: Proposals for Solution

Leonidas Chrysanthopoulos, as a career diplomat, participated in the negotiations for the accession of Greece to the European Economic Community. He has served as consul general in Istanbul, minister-counsellor in Beijing, and at the mission of Greece to the UN. He was the first Greek ambassador to Armenia and was ambassador to Poland and Canada. Ambassador Chrysanthopoulos was director general of EU affairs in the Ministry of Foreign Affairs and from 2006 to 2012, he was the elected Secre-

tary General of the Black Sea Economic Cooperation Organization (BSEC). He is currently active in the Unified Popular Front (EPAM) to liberate Greece from the "memoranda" regime of Eu-imposed austerity. He is the author of The Caucasus Chronicles: Nation Building and Diplomacy in Armenia.

Allow me at the outset to congratulate the Schiller Institute and its Director, Helga Zepp-La-Rouche, for trying to make the world better for humanity. I wish us all success in this important conference and hope that the outcome will be beneficial for us all.

The theme of our conference is very appropriate and comes at a moment when humanity is not only facing its worst economic crisis since the depression of 1928, but also the worst refugee crisis since the Second World War, due to the aggressive policies of the United States in the last decade, that have destroyed Afghanistan, Iraq, Libya, and Syria. The EU is continuing to gradually collapse, as it destroys its member states, forcing some to consider leaving, while its democratic deficit is increasing and far-right parties are closing in on power.

The world economy cannot get out of a vicious circle that it has been in since the outset of the crisis in 2008. We are witnessing global demonstrations against austerity measures that enhance poverty instead of growth, and against greedy financial systems that lead to extreme social inequality. The demonstrations in France are a good example. Until now, nobody has been listening to the people. It is due time that decisions be taken on priorities beneficial to the interests of human beings. We should no longer ask the question of what the markets are saying, but what our people are saying.

The EU not only has become an incompetent organization, but is also in disarray as more and more is being heard every day about political parties with right-wing programs, and exiting the EU. The UK referendum of Thursday demonstrates the case.

In Greece the situation is deteriorating. After the legislation adopted by Parliament on May 22, Greece has ceased to exist as a state, having given the economic management of the country to the lenders and to the EU for the next 100 years. It is the first time in history that a country has dissolved itself. Parliament will no longer have any role to play in this area. In May 2010, the Greek government was forced to sign the Loan Agreement so that it could, through austerity measures, reduce the public debt which in 2009 was 129% of GNP or 299 billion euro in absolute numbers. After three memoranda and the mistaken policies of the EU, the IMF, and the Greek governments, not only was the public debt not reduced, but it has increased to 180% of GNP.

The Syriza government was elected on an anti-austerity program, yet betrayed the Greek people by doing exactly the opposite. It did not even take into account a referendum in which 62% of the people voted against the austerity measures. In spite of the fact that they had acknowledged their mistakes, the EU, the European Central Bank, and the IMF continue to insist on the implementation of the same ineffective policies that are destroying a member-state of the EU and its people. Unemployment is up to 25% from 9% in 2010, Greeks looking into garbage bins for food is a common sight, overtaxation has paralyzed the economy, and the health system has collapsed, while more than 5,000 people have committed suicide.

But it is not only that the measures are erroneous, they have also violated the Lisbon Treaty as well as the human rights of the Greek people, something that is also mentioned in the report dated February 29 of the UN independent expert, Juan Pablo Bohoslavski, to the UN Human Rights Council:

> The U.S.-provoked war in Syria with the participation of some EU states has created the biggest refugee crisis since World War II. Almost 5 million refugees have left Syria to ask asylum mainly in the EU. Germany has 484,000, Sweden 108.000 and more in other Member States. Turkey is currently hosting 2,748,000, Lebanon 1,500,000 and Jordan 1,265,000. The EU, once the champion of humanitarian assistance, was incapable of managing the refugee flow. Greece, a country that had no participation in the Syrian war, was inundated with an increased number of refugees while many of its Central European members refused to accept them. Though the movements into Greece were gradually reduced after the shaky EU-Turkey Agreement of March the EU has still to live up to its previous decisions, according to which 60,000 refugees from Greece and Italy would be resettled in EU member-states. Today, Greece has 56,000 refugees, all of whom want to depart North. It is, however a shame that the US has accepted only 4,000 refugees.

Another threat facing humanity is the U.S. animosity towards Russia, as if we were still in the cold war period. A missile system is being set up to encircle Russia and, of course, Moscow is preparing a defense shield to counter it. The EU embargo on Russia after the Ukrainian crisis is not at all helping the situation. Also, threats have been recently made by Obama against China with references to the need to restrict her economic power.

With a collapsing EU and a United States looking for confrontation with Russia and China, a solution for humanity can be the BRICS' initiative. This is an initiative of Brazil, Russia, India, China, and South Africa to pursue a policy of economic development for the benefit of humanity. They created their own Development Bank to invest in necessary development projects. China has also established the Asian Infrastructure Investment Bank, joined by over 20 Asian nations as founding members, and has set up a Silk Road Development Fund. Within the BRICS, China has proposed the creation of a Free Trade Area of Asia and the Pacific. The Chinese proposal was quickly rejected by Obama, who created his own free trade organization. The incorporation of the Shanghai Cooperation Agreement to the BRICS could create a formidable power, which—if remaining out of the control of the bankers—could be decisive so that humanity reaches global peace and ends poverty through economic development.

From what was previously mentioned, we can see that there is a crisis of civilization that is impeding humanity's progress. I totally agree with the Schiller Institute's viewpoint that we need a renaissance of Classical culture, as we see measures being taken to prevent it from happening. Not only is the educational system in Greece doing everything possible to make Classical culture disappear,— it seems to be following steps taken in the United States and in other EU countries. It seems that Classical culture, which also encompasses humanism, philosophy, the sciences, and art, creates fear among the ruling classes who do not want to see the people thinking again. We should resist any such tendencies.

As for the dialogue of cultures,— yes by all means this should take place, and perhaps we could get on board the UN dialogue of civilizations and make it even better. Both dialogues are useful efforts to enhance efforts for a permanent global peace.

In conclusion, and after having criticized the EU and the United States, allow me to propose some solutions that would be beneficial for humanity.

Greece. For Greece it is imperative to denounce the Loan Facility Agreement of May 2010, on the basis of Articles 8-52 of the Vienna Convention concerning the Law of Treaties. These articles anticipate the invalidity of a treaty, if there was error, fraud, or coercion of a representative of a state. The cessation of payments with the denunciation of the Loan Agreement and the nationalization of the Bank of Greece, will allow Greece to repair the damage done and instigate true development. Adoption of a national currency will follow. The Unified Popular Front (EPAM), a political party not in parliament yet, supports such a policy.

The EU. There must be a transformation of the EU into an efficient organization, having as its sole priority the safeguarding of the interests of its people. A new charter is necessary, drafted by movements of citizens of member-states who will submit their proposals to a European Assembly composed of representatives of these movements. The existing EU must be dissolved.

The United States. It must stop its policy of destroying nations, and Obama must return to the Nobel Committee the Peace Prize that was awarded to him, since he did nothing to deserve it.(The same applies to the EU, which also received the Peace Prize.) The United States must adopt a more friendly policy towards Russia and the rest of the world, for the benefit of humanity.

Humanity. The deletion of the global debt, which is about $600 trillion, will allow humanity to restart on a new and healthy basis. In history, we have examples of debt deletion, from the ancient Greek Sisahthia to the Jubilee of ancient Hebrew communities, where every 50 years all debts were cancelled. Even during the 1970s, the developed countries of the West deleted the debt of the Non-Aligned Movement, thus allowing the economic boom of Yugoslavia. The BRICS' movement can promote this while the decision must be taken by the G-8. Humanity as a whole will benefit, because it will be able to restart on sound and healthy principles.

In order to implement the previously mentioned proposals, it is necessary to have politicians with imagination, vision, and courage—politicians who care about the progress of humanity and who can control the greed of multinational companies by restricting their power. Such politicians do not exist today. So we have to create them.

The New Paradigm Represented by the 'One Belt, One Road' Policy

REN LIN

The New Silk Road Win-Win Perspective

Dr. Ren Lin is a researcher on the One Belt, One Road policy, at the Chinese Academy of Social Sciences.

Dr. Ren said that the Brexit vote shocked her, as much of what she has been researching for the One Belt, One Road (OBOR) policy is on how to make globalization work. "I favor integration," she said. "Cooperation through OBOR is a form of globalization."

She then reviewed the challenges presented by globalization, and how the OBOR policy addresses them. For example, challenges such as eliminating poverty, can industry be reconstructed (after the effects of free trade lowering wages), and dealing with geopolitical issues which threaten security.

After reviewing ten such challenges, she said that the solution lies in precisely the way China is pursuing the OBOR policy. The best way to resolve regional and cross-regional problems is to cooperate, with infrastructure projects. In describing the win-win policy, she said that "complementarity" is the only proper approach, where stronger countries use their advantages to help others, not to compete against them.

There can be no unilateral solutions, she added, and policies must be based on acting globally, with every interest in mind. There must be inclusive institutions, such as the Asian Infrastructure Investment Bank (AIIB), which can bring people together around mutual concerns. The OBOR, she concluded, is "an open project, not a finalized plan." Other nations—referring to European nations and the United States, in particular—can join in, to overcome global problems.

EIR will publish a full transcript of Dr. Ren's remarks.

HAMID SADIG

Greetings to the Conference from the Ambassador of Afghanistan to Germany

H.E. Hamid Sidig is Ambassador and Extraordinary Representative of the Islamic Republic of Afghanistan to Germany.

Dear Mrs. Zepp-LaRouche, dear Colleagues and Friends:

I would like to express my gratitude and honor to be part of this important event. Over the past 30 years, the Schiller Institute has played a significant role in promoting international discussions on major topics that have shaped the future of our world.

Since ancient times the Silk Road has been a symbol of the commercial artery that connects Asia and Europe, creating wealth and cultural exchange to benefit all countries involved.

Our conference today hopes to build on this ancient tradition by bringing together scientists and politicians to develop a New Silk Road and begin the process of healing and regenerating this region.

Our vision is to create a secure and peaceful life for our region, which will allow thousands of refugees to return back to their homes and rebuild their communities.

This conference shall look at the possibilities of how we can create such a future: a future based on eco-

nomic, social, political, and cultural cooperation; that will bring stability and prosperity to Eurasia which is so desperately needed. We should not forget the most important issue of security and the harboring of elements that are destabilizing the entire region.

I believe that we should work to build an infrastructure and pathways to facilitate this vision through trade.

On a practical level, we need to build new railroads, including high-speed train links; look at new sources of green and secure energy; and explore new technologies and innovations, particularly in IT, to facilitate our success; and finally establish fair trade agreements to compete in global markets.

Our ancestors, with their limited technologies and standards, were able to sustain this important trade link for more than a millennium. Today, we should be capable not only of rebuilding it, but of making it the economic and cultural highway for the next millennium.

If we envision a better future today, together we can make it a reality for tomorrow.

Ladies and gentlemen, I thank you for your attention.

EGBERT DREWS

International Networking in the Economy: Practical Experience

Egbert Drews is a board member of MARWIKO, AG, Berlin, an alliance of medium-sized companies operating in the international economy.

Ladies and Gentlemen,

I would like to thank Mrs. Zepp-LaRouche and the organizers of this conference for the opportunity to speak to you. You may be surprised to hear it, but as business entrepreneurs of the *Mittelstand* or SME [small and medium-sized enterprises], we are related to the subject of this conference, and we are very much interested in this debate and in the development of this idea. I shall attempt, in my contribution, to present how this theme affects us on the basis of our experience.

Given the globalization and liberalization of the economy, the significance of cooperation among SMEs has considerably grown over the past years: The SMEs recognize that this approach is a means of achieving the needed growth potential, which they cannot realize by themselves due to a lack of or insufficient financial resources, market share or competencies.

Cooperation often affords a much more flexible and more effective approach in the short term for common growth than mergers or acquisitions. Essentially, this involves organizing cooperation at different stages of the value chain, such as project identification, marketing, implementation, and funding, aimed at bundling specific competencies and resources to find and then exploit market potentials.

That is precisely the core activity of our enterprise. MARWIKO AG offers mainly medium-sized enterprises new lines of business or additional strategies for their portfolios, and today they primarily involve cross-border business transactions.

As an international consortium of medium-sized companies, MARWIKO AG operates a wide-ranging network, which makes it the reference point for partners through extensive contacts in important economic regions of the world. Its foundation is good contacts and a well-run international network.

Mittelstand Cooperation

We present an unbureaucratic, practical instrument for different types of cooperation among *Mittelstand* firms—a platform that brings companies together both physically and electronically, harmonizes their activities, and develops opportunities for synergies.

We operate an active cooperation management, which means—

• Integration of a cooperation partner into the actual activity of the company;

• Active search for offers, projects, partners, and regions supported by that partner, and concrete support based on MARWIKO's structures and network;

• Transfer of selected activities into MARWIKO's portfolio;

• Bundling of the partner's offers and competencies in the regions and on the projects by MARWIKO; and

• Presentations by the partner at trade fairs and exhibitions, project trips, and other activities.

Success is only possible under conditions that are advantageous for all and with the acceptance of the partners. That presents the immediate relation to the model of cooperation among States.

In the preamble to this panel, it says:

"China, with the New Silk Road policy, has put a completely different model of cooperation on the agenda, based on 'win-win' cooperation, which is consciously focused on the interests of the other. With the New Silk Road, the Maritime Silk Road, and a series of new financial institutions designed solely to finance the real economy, an alternative is already in place, which over 60 nations now consider to be a more attractive model."

In our opinion, the future of countries and their successful economic development lies in the commitment to common grounds in the coordination of their political principles for a national economic development policy which is anchored in an advantageous development for all regions, that is dominated by none.

The central themes for German *Mittelstand*—according to the Federal Economics Ministry—are internationally competitive funding for starting-up and growth, the successful handling of company successions, assured availability of skilled staff, relief from bureaucracy, and digitalization so that German SMEs can remain vital, strong, and innovative in meeting the challenges.

The themes are, among others, to:
• Promote entrepreneurial spirit;
• Support the availability of a future skilled workforce;
• Use and design digitalization; and
• Strengthen innovations.

Mittelstand entrepreneurs know better than anyone else that, in these areas, they have a great potential of their own and can essentially carry out these tasks themselves. But that is not the case in the field of *Mittelstand* and Globalization.

"The Federal Ministry assumes that the volume of world trade will nearly quadruple by the year 2030. On this backdrop, even more *Mittelstand* entrepreneurs should regard globalization as an opportunity. To make the move to markets abroad, the Ministry provides foreign trade promotion, which is continually expanded in cooperation with the business world and which should become even better known among companies."

As for the performance of the German *Mittelstand,* the figures speak clearly. Over 99% of all companies are small and medium-sized companies, over 82% of all apprentices are trained there, and they provide nearly 60% of all jobs. Fifty-six percent of our economic output is produced in SMEs. But we should not lose sight of the actual conditions the *Mittelstand* is exposed to.

The Ministry also assumes that *"The takedown of trade restrictions . . . should benefit SMEs in particular. Therefore, the Ministry is committed to trade facilitation and the conclusion of bilateral and multilateral free trade agreements."*

According to the estimates of the EU Commission and the German government, SMEs should benefit from a large portion of the assumed growth. We believe that the positive impact of the Transatlantic Trade and Investment Partnership (TTIP) on SMEs is overestimated, and that, critically assessed, the risks greatly outweigh the opportunities.

Until March 2015, the EU Commission, the government, the employers' association, and the Chambers of Commerce claimed that TTIP would bring significant gains in growth and income, as well as hundreds of thousands of jobs to the EU, and cited to that effect the relevant studies. But the estimates, including in the EU-commissioned studies, could not be confirmed.

The positive effects, if there are any, will only appear among those SMEs that export onto the world market. Given the SMEs' strong orientation to regional sales markets, only 7% of them turn up as exporters in the foreign trade statistics.

Among the top leaders of the export-oriented industries, such as production industry, services, trade and transport, that account for some 68% of the German gross value added, SMEs only have an export quota of 4% to 20%. Also, in trade with the United States, SMEs play only a small role.

The TTIP

According to a publication of the Hamburg Chamber of Commerce, only 950 companies have business relations with the United States, which is less than one percent of all the companies registered at the Chamber.

German SMEs in the production industry are mostly specialized providers of high-quality products with strong innovative capabilities. That implies a corresponding level of prices. If the current quality standards are lowered through the harmonization of standards in the "domestic market" of the TTIP space, and if public instruments of protection are considered to be trade restrictions and therefore eliminated, then transnational competitors, who have the advantage of economies of scale, would be able to oust middle-sized innovators from the market through a low-price strategy which is more or less harmless for them. In such cases, an active public regulatory policy should be provided for the *Mittelstand*, but that would be considered a non-tariff barrier and therefore would violate the TTIP.

That free-trade agreements such as the TTIP are generally advantageous for transnational companies and detrimental for SMEs, can be seen in the experience with the North American Free Trade Agreement

(NAFTA), which went into effect in 1994. In the 20 years since then, in Canada, the share of the largest listed corporations of total profit nearly doubled, while the major macroeconomic indicators were cut in half in the same time period. In the agricultural sector in particular, the SMEs were heavily disadvantaged.

So far, according to the Restriction of Competition Act (GWB), medium-sized companies should be handled preferentially when awarding public contracts. But in view of the expected principle of non-discrimination in awarding community contracts, it is to be expected that the practice will change to the detriment of SMEs and that in the future, only corporations still active internationally will take part in such tenders, because of their logistical and operational advantages.

According to the figures published by the Federal Statistics Office in 2012, German foreign trade with the BRICS countries (Brazil, Russia, India, China, South Africa) increased nearly sevenfold, while the entire foreign trade only grew twofold.

It would be disastrous for the export-oriented SMEs if those markets were destroyed by the thrust of the so-called free trade agreement (FTA) between the EU and the United States which the EU Commission intends to impose. But that is exactly the effect the EU Commission expects and describes, since it considers China, India, and the member states of the Association of South East Asian Nations (ASEAN) as the losers of the so-called FTA. Thus, German exporters represented in the foreign trade association BGA warn against a kind of "Economic NATO" at the expense of other trade partners. But that seems to be the intention of the German policy, when the geopolitical and geostrategic advantages of a bilateral agreement between the EU and the United States are mentioned, which is meant to set the standards before they can be set by China, India, or the alliance of the BRICS.

In our opinion, these are economic policy strategies on a geopolitical background. We are convinced that in the 21st Century other approaches are needed, which are rather reflected in the model of cooperation initiated by China.

Upon weighing the claimed opportunities and the expected consequences of TTIP, it is not surprising that a clear majority of the small and medium-sized companies, according to a poll by the Federal Association of SMEs (BVMW), are critical toward the TTIP negotiations. Although this group is not known for ideological or anti-business prejudice, its attitude toward the FTA is conspicuously critical.

As small and medium-sized entrepreneurs, we are for fair, transparent free trade on the basis of high environmental and social standards. The planned FTA with the United States (TTIP) contradicts those principles.

Core elements of the planned agreement, such as the Investor State Dispute Settlement (ISDS), the harmonization of norms and standards, as well as deregulation in the fields of culture, services for the public, and public tenders, benefit mainly the interests of global corporations with more capital and more staff, that will force the SMEs out of the market.

Germany, Russia, China

At the same time, we are very concerned that the attempt of the EU and the United States to define international trade rules on their own, can lead to the disruption of the economic order and thereby jeopardize essential markets for us in the emerging countries (BRICS and others). As we know, over 2,000 German medium-sized entrepreneurs have signed a petition against the agreement.

We, as small entrepreneurs, assume our responsibility for society, and we value high social and ecological standards in Europe as well as vibrant democracy and a functioning constitutional state.

The European domestic market has become much more important for SMEs: over 93% of SME exports go to the European market. Therefore, the interests of SMEs in an SME-friendly domestic market and the takedown of unjustified restrictions must be represented with a stronger voice in Brussels. We need a just balance between growing market integration and the preservation of proven, successful structures, in particular self-management of the economy and its core elements, such as dual occupational training, master craftsmanship certificates, representative chambers, and social partnership.

We followed with great interest the visit of EU Commission President Jean-Claude Juncker to the St. Petersburg International Economic Forum, and we see it as a step in the right direction. The Committee on Eastern European Economic Relations also welcomed Juncker's participation in the Forum, saying it is time to begin a dialogue between the EU and the Eurasian Economic Union concerning a common economic space from Lisbon to Vladivostok. It could begin by harmonizing standards and lowering trade restriction, according to the committee's President, Wolfgang Büchele.

As a consortium of the SMEs, we see hope and perspectives in a new type of economic cooperation among countries. It is difficult enough, but also interesting, to carry out economic cooperation in other cultures. We are competent and experienced in this job and we know what we need—respect, tolerance, and mutual benefit.

That was again proven in the tenth Business Day that my company organized in Berlin during the German-Russian celebrations. Over one hundred companies from Germany and Russia responded to our invitation. This format of mutual exchanges, contacts, and discussions about fruitful cooperation of companies is very much appreciated by SMEs, and we like to use it as a platform for cooperation.

We are not competing in any way with your conference; we are only concerned with the clear economic interests of our partners and their development for mutual benefit.

We will organize a similar Business Day in October after our next trip to China. We already see synergies and cooperative opportunities not only among our partners, but also in the triangle of relations among Germany, Russia, and China. We believe that is the right approach in the spirit of your conference.

I thank you again for the Schiller Institute's Initiative and wish you great success in the process of rethinking cooperation in politics and the economy.

MICHEL RAIMBAUD

In Syria, Against the War Party, Build Peace and International Law

Michel Raimbaud is a former French ambassador, particularly in the Arab world, Africa, and Latin America. He is the former director of the French Office for Protection of Refugees and Stateless Persons (OFPRA). He titled his address, "In Syria and Elsewhere, Against the War Party and the Law of the Jungle, Rebuild Peace with Respect for International Law."

The world today faces a great danger of war, more than ever before. It is going through a global crisis.

One hears much talk about a new cold war that would lead us back to the old confrontation between the "Free World," the ancestor of the "Axis of Good," and a "totalitarian bloc," dubbed the "Axis of Evil" by George Bush, a confrontation which ended with the victory of the United States over communism.

The disappearance of the U.S.S.R. in 1991, which Vladimir Putin called the "greatest geopolitical catastrophe of the 20th century," provoked the rise of the famous "unipolar American moment" of sinister memory—a much shorter moment than expected by the At-

lantic Empire, which thought it would be eternal, but much too long for the rest of the planet, especially for the poorest among us.

"The most powerful empire the world has ever seen," "more powerful than Rome" is what the indispensable and unique hyperpower was for 20 years (1991 to 2011), as it assumed the vocation of dominating the world, in the name of a messianism inspired both by the Old and the New Testaments. This alleged "divine will," that is, the whims of the new masters of the world, took the place of International Law. It is upon the rubble of that legality that the American imperial order was built, around a "civilized center" erecting itself as the "international community," attempting to rule the planet, including a number of peripheral rogue states.

The Elizabeth Arden Club (Washington, London, and Paris) has claimed for a quarter of a century that it embodies the "international community." It is a political directorate inspired by that war party, whose followers make up the "Deep State" of Western and other countries. Some speak of "the military-industrial complex"; others call it the "neo-conservative" current. That bellicose, imperial party, interventionist and bigoted, carries out, in the name of God, a systematic policy of aggression, interventionism, destruction,— a criminal policy. Their aim is supposedly to impose peace, democracy and human rights throughout the world, in particular in the Arab-Muslim world, including and especially through force, since it is the divine will of the Empire to do Good and repress Evil (by the way, that is the name of the religious police of the Wahhabite Saudi regime). NATO is the armed branch of that war party, of the Atlantic Empire.

The Atlanticist leaders move in the shadows, hiding behind the false flags of democracy, justice, morality, and law. They demonize any country that opposes their ambitions by calling them to the Gehenna of "worrying states" to be carved up into "democratic" entities: In short, they are "rogue states." That concept has played an essential role in U.S. strategy for several decades, and it is by evoking this bogeyman, that they have systematically violated and destroyed International Law.

That Law is based on the United Nations Charter which, in Article 51, attributes solely to the Security Council, the right to take the adequate measures it deems necessary to maintain peace and international security. But the neocons in Washington couldn't care less about UN legality.

The only thing that counts is threats to American interests, which make "direct military interventions" necessary. For them, the law is not founded on the UN Charter, but on the U.S. constitution. According to Noam Chomsky, "that contempt of the primacy of law is profoundly imbedded in American culture and practices."

The neoconservative doctrine, the "zero degree of political thought," has a simple basis: The Cold war is finished, but the United States still has the responsibility to protect the world from "rogue states." In the 1970s, Nixon thought that the United States should give the impression that it was ruled by "madmen with unpredictable behavior, armed with a huge potential of destruction, in order to create or reinforce the fears of its adversaries (madman theory)." Annals of United States strategy show that those evaluations are not pure fantasy.

In August 1990, Washington and London decreed that Iraq was a rogue state, and it became the first of a long list: Sudan, Afghanistan, Somalia, Palestine, Yugoslavia, Iran, and Ukraine, followed by others, including Syria (2011). In June 2000, Robert McNamara, the former American Defense Secretary (1961-1968), told the *International Herald Tribune* that the United States

had become a rogue state. Noam Chomsky said the same in the beginning of the "Arab springs," noting that his country put itself above international law.

The War Party

The world in 2016 is no longer that of the Cold War, but it is also different from what it was in 2011. Like all the adages on matters of war and peace, the Latin expression, "*Si vis pacem, para bellum*" (If you wish for peace, prepare for war), is ambiguous, because it raises the concept of armed peace. Yet this is the motto of the War College in France, and of the British navy. It could very well be the motto of NATO. The Romans, claiming they were harassed by the barbarians, decided to declare war on them in order to distract their attention, and to be able to enjoy the famous *Pax Romana* in their own empire. Some cynical minds believe that the message is indeed: "If you want peace at home, make war against others." This is the meaning given to the expression by the leaders and thinkers of the war party.

Today, a peace camp is opposed to the war party. The Peace camp refers to principles of International Law, to crisis settlement through negotiations and to the perspective of a multipolar world, as opposed to the War party which prospers on the rubble of the UN legality, imposing chaos, the law of the jungle, and seeking every occasion to impose its views by force.

Whether it is the wars in the Middle East, the threats of nuclear conflict, the coming implosion of the financial system, the refugee crisis, or other dramas that afflict the planet, you never have to look too far to find the hawks ready to do everything to preserve the hegemony of the Atlantic camp, if need be by war, and to stop the world from changing. To reconcile beautiful principles and noble values on the one hand, with wars of aggression and criminal behavior on the other, the chaos theory manual has an answer.

Yet the Nuremberg Tribunal, which knew what it was talking about, ordained that "to launch a war of aggression ... is not only an international crime; it is the supreme international crime differing only from other war crimes in that it contains within itself the accumulated evil of the whole."

The debate about ethics in international relations is loaded. It is a real debate for some, a smoke screen for others; the reference to legality does not have the same value for both camps. Diplomats cannot work miracles if they have only indefensible policies to defend, on the wrong side of history. They cannot be constructive if they act in the service of destructive leaders, determined to continue the war and to weaken diplomacy.

Master of the Empire, the United States carries the main responsibility for those crimes, destructions, and atrocities we have just mentioned. Obama boasts that he avoided the worst in August 2013, by deciding not to launch punitive strikes against Syria in the wake of the chemical weapons affair. In fact, the decision to break the rules of the game seems to have been more motivated by his desire to affirm his own power against the Chiefs of Staff, the secret services, and the think tanks, that are all under the influence of, and financed by Saudi Arabia and other Middle Eastern countries, and most of which work for the Arab or pro-Israeli financiers.

Nothing would prompt the peoples of the Greater Middle East to disagree with Paul Craig Roberts, the former U.S. Assistant Treasury Secretary, when he wrote with his vitriolic pen (*Le Blog de la Résistance*, January 12, 2016): "Unique among the countries on Earth, ... the U.S. government is the most complete criminal organization in human history."

Despite his smiles and lovely speeches, Obama has lit and kept going more conflicts than George W. Bush, and he is heading a state responsible for the death of millions of children and adults, the destruction of states and of whole societies, tens of millions of lives broken, without even having to go all the way back to Hiroshima and Nagasaki. Having continued to wreak havoc in the Greater Middle East, he has contributed more than anyone to nuclear proliferation, especially in Europe, and to relaunching a war of aggression against Russia and China. Words full of peace, but acts of war galore.

An Uncompromising Future

Supported by the Zionist lobby, the Saudis and the Gulf countries, by the weapons dealers, the financial groups and the favorite candidate of the neo-conservative camp, Hillary Clinton, Obama's former Secretary of State, has a long record as a war-monger and extremist. She has played an active role in fanning the flames of all conflicts and wars for a quarter of a century now: Yugoslavia, Kosovo, Libya, and Syria, not to mention Ukraine and Honduras in between. An enthusiastic proponent of "regime change," she is wildly anti-Syrian, anti-Iranian, anti-Hezbollah, anti-Russian, and anti-Chinese. And wildly pro-Israeli as well.

Paradoxically, there are many wise people on the other side of the Atlantic who hope that Donald Trump will be elected, since his isolationism might steer Washington off the course of war-like interventionism.

The vassals of the Empire, whether Europeans, Middle Eastern, or others, are accomplices and co-responsible for all the suffering perpetrated. It is common knowledge that France and its NATO allies, with their privileged relationships to Qatar, Saudi Arabia, Turkey and Israel, have played a key role in the "supreme international crime" which is wars of aggression; it was the case in Syria as in Libya before. That support is multiple and accepted: closing down of embassies, sanctions, active support to the armed opposition, including terrorists, activism at the UN Security Council, deployment of special forces in flagrant violation of international law (June 2016), tolerance toward jihadists leaving for Syria.

The Current State of Affairs

In 2011, it was Syria's turn. It had long been targeted by the Empire, both by the Israeli-American plans to break it up, and by the measures and statements adopted since 2001. We will not go into the details here.

The Syrian state has not collapsed, as its "friends" expected. It pays wages and pensions to its civil servants without default, its institutions are in place, and its constitutional calendar has been respected, all things taken into account. Its national army, supported by the Russian, Iranian, and Lebanese (Hezbollah) allies, has resisted an aggression of the great western powers in alliance with the fundamentalists of the Middle East and tens of thousands of mercenaries of a hundred nationalities.

Two-thirds of Syria has been destroyed, after five years of savage violence during which it served as a testing ground for all forms of "creative chaos." A country formerly prosperous, self-sufficient, and debt-free, with functioning public services and free education and healthcare, lies today in ruins. Its infrastructure (schools, hospitals, social centers, roads) is destroyed. To achieve that result, the aggressors, claiming to be "friends of Syria," had to help the terrorists of the armed opposition break a good part of the country.

The multi-form sanctions had an impact on the Syrian national fabric, united by an exemplary "secular tolerance," but were not able to destroy it. The aim of this politicide was, and is still, to demoralize the populations, while creating the illusion that the West is there to "save them from the tyrant who is massacring them," and to welcome the refugees and turncoats.

Just in the year July 2011-July 2012, the EU and the United States, Canada, and Australia, launched 17 different sets of sanctions ... The diplomatic sanctions were adopted starting Autumn 2011, after Russia and China vetoed the UN Security Council draft resolution inspired by the Libyan precedent.

The human costs are extremely heavy. With 300 to 400,000 dead (of which at least 130,000 were soldiers of the regular army), more than one million handicapped, 14 million refugees or displaced people (more than one out of two Syrians), the nation's fabric is torn, weakened by the proliferation of armed groups and by the invasion of mercenaries joining the jihad, and by certain ethnic demands.

Immense Material Damages

For Syria alone, recent estimates put at $300 billion the cost of destruction and looting. Bernard Cornut, a Middle East expert, wrote on March 11 2016, "Given that it is increasingly known and proven that several countries—France, the U.S.A., Great Britain, and of course Qatar, Saudi Arabia, Turkey—supported and financed the armed rebel groups with the stated and shared aim of changing the regime, and notably to oust the elected president, those countries, and others that Syria knows, are all co-responsible to different degrees for the damages incurred, estimated recently at $1 trillion." And he concluded, "they will have to deal with actions taken by Syria in international courts to obtain legitimate war claims." He proposes to create a tax on oil and gas, which would be used for a "fund to compensate victims and reconstruct Syria," to be managed by the UN.

The horrendous count in Iraq—one and a half million dead, of whom 500,000 were children—is there to remind us that sanctions are a weapon of mass destruction, used with total cynicism by the "masters of the world." For Madeleine Albright, "it was worth it."

The upheavals of the past years (according to Canadian expert Ahmed Ben Saada), in terms of "Arab Springs" led to 1.5 million dead and wounded, and more than 15 million refugees and displaced persons.

For all the Arab countries, they caused losses on the order of $833 billion ($300 billion just for Syria) of which more than one half were damage to infrastructure and archeological or historical sites. Let us add to those pharaonic devastations, financed by the oil-producing states to the tune of tens of billions, the hundreds of billions of dollars "frozen" (in other terms, "stolen") by the sanctions (plus $700 billion for Libya).

Politically, the future of Syria is not yet sealed, as *realpolitik* keeps knocking on the door of the over-optimistic analysts. The armed jihadi opponents had a hard time disguising themselves as negotiators; their record would more easily lead them to the International Criminal Court than towards diplomatic tasks. But their Western mentors think they have some virtues: their protégés refuse to negotiate from a weak position. From time to time, they need a ceasefire to reconstitute themselves. If they violate the truce it doesn't matter, the one to blame is the Bashar al Assad "regime." This vicious circle is self-feeding, as politicians, journalists, and Western intellectuals all take part, with a few exceptions, in the conspiracy of lies.

The military situation weighs heavily in the diplomatic balance. At this end of June 2016, it is manifest that NATO, in all illegality, is setting up a deployment in the north of Syria the purpose of which—the fight against Daesh—is either a bad joke or a new war.

Rebuild Peace with Respect for Law

To rebuild peace with respect for law, we must reconstruct legality and rediscover the UN principles (sovereignty of states, non-interventionism, obligation to negotiate to solve conflicts) by introducing a new paradigm: the BRICS can be that new paradigm, which tends to usher in a new type of relations respectful of sovereignties and mutually profitable.

Reconstruction cannot be conceived along the lines of a classical scheme: a pool of financiers, emanating from the West, and a Syria at the mercy of the "benefactor" which destroyed it. The United States and NATO are hardly suited to solving crises, since they were the instigators.

This is why the project launched by China, called "the New Silk Roads: a Belt and a Road," responds to the expectations of numerous countries, close to 70 today. We will not go into the presentation of our Chinese colleague.

That project, which integrates a good part of the Greater Middle East, notably Syria and its neighbors (Iran, Lebanon, and Iraq), as well as its allies (Russia, China) in a vast ensemble of win-win economic cooperation, could shake up the regional balances, reorient trade, and break the logic of a dominant North versus a dominated South. In the end, that means some 900 projects, and financial contributions close to $900 billion, as Helga Zepp-LaRouche recalled it.

That project could rebuild a destroyed Syria on a new basis, respecting its freedom of choice and free of any threats. It aims at ensuring a more stable environment, knowing that South West Asia is structured around two corridors (with major roles for Iran, Iraq, Syria, Saudi Arabia, and Turkey), whether the railway corridor (axis launched in 2011) or the road corridor (from Urumqi in Xinjiang to the Near East) or the maritime corridor leading to the Mediterranean through the Suez Canal.

The Schiller Institute, for its part, proposes a project in line with the same perspective: "The New Silk Road Becomes the World Land-Bridge," which also bases itself on a change of rules of the world economy while reserving a specific role for the reconstruction of Southwest Asia, ravaged by war and conflicts for a quarter of a century now, but holding an enormous potential of development and immense natural and human resources, which explain for geopoliticians the lust of the Eurasian countries and the Empires of the Sea.

That project echoes the strategy of "five seas" announced by President Bashar al Assad in 2004, for the creation of a network of infrastructure between the Mediterranean, the Indian Ocean, the Red Sea, the Caspian Sea and the Black Sea, aimed at making of this strategic hinge zone, an area of exchanges among the three continents of the ancient world.

There Will Be a Reconstruction

Obviously, there will be a reconstruction.

1. However, the terrorist groups supported by the West and their allies will have to stop their destructions. It would suffice for that, that the existing resolutions of the Security Council be applied.

2. There will be no reconstruction without rapidly lifting the sanctions whose object is the destruction of a people and their country.

3. The solution is not to receive in Europe the refugees which have been created in one way or the other by fanning the flames of a war of aggression and jihad in Syria.

4. On the other hand, the struggle against Daesh, while certainly a priority, is not an end in itself, because it will not solve all Syria's problems, especially in its future as a resisting nation state.

It is up to the Syrian people and only up to them to decide Syria's destiny, without foreign intervention. It is that principle of sovereignty that Chinese President Xi Jinping brings forth when he claims the end of the Unipolar area and that the world is now multipolar. Vladimir Putin has also placed himself within the framework of an international legality and supports the Syrian state and "the armed forces of President Al Assad which are the only ones really fighting the Islamic state." The Russian president's decisions to intervene provoke anger among the Westerners, furious at his continual references to an international law that they violate.

BOUTHAINA SHAABAN

Reconstruction with Syrian Characteristics

H.E. Dr. Bouthaina Shaaban, Presidency of the Syrian Arab Republic, delivered her address by means of a video recording titled, "Reconstruction with Syrian Characteristics: Rebuilding a Truly Diverse and More Secure World Based on the Lessons of the Syrian Experience." After the playing of her video, she joined the conference by Skype to answer questions. The transcript of her address is followed here by notes of the discussion by Skype.

Good morning.

Allow me first to thank the Schiller Institute, and in particular, to thank Helga Zepp-LaRouche, for inviting me to this very important conference and for allowing me to contribute to this very important panel.

But before I begin my paper, I would like to pass on a few notes that lead me to the conclusion which I would love to conclude for this panel, and for this conference at large.

One of the major problems we face in our country, is that today, Western countries approach our countries with the feeling of exceptionalism or a feeling of righteousness, that whatever Western countries see appropriate or good, should apply to our countries without any question. The first action that was taken by Western countries, when the war on Syria started, was to withdraw their ambassadors from Syria. The question is, isn't it the job of the ambassadors to convey the reality on the ground, and to help in opening channels of communication between countries instead of closing them?

This leads me to the role of corporate media during the war on Syria. Unfortunately, most Western media rely on *Al Jazeera*, Qatar-funded, and *Al Arabiya*, Saudi-funded, to report on events in Syria, even though both channels, *Al Jazeera* and *Al Arabiya*, withdrew their correspondents and relied on what are called "eyewitnesses," which could be anybody, anywhere. This applies also to the Syrian Observatory for Human Rights, which is run by one person in Coventry, U.K., Rami Abdel Rahman.

These media outlets choose to focus on what they find which fits their agenda, ignoring the reality on the ground. For example, even the terrorist acts in Tartus and Jableh recently, which claimed the lives of 200 innocent civilians, were not noticed by Western media, and certainly did not therefore evoke any Western sympathy.

What I would like to say is that the false narrative propagated about Syria was as dangerous to the Syrian people and to the safety and security of Syrians, as the acts perpetrated by terrorists, because it isolated the reality in Syria from the public understanding in the West and in the world at large, and it prevented the creation of a level of understanding between Western countries and the Syrian people about what is going on.

Terrorism and 'Democracy'

But before we can begin to talk about reconstructing Syria, we still face the monumental challenge of eradicating terrorism in Syria, Iraq, and the region. We have to eradicate this terrorism. And when I say "we,"

I do not mean the Syrians or the Iraqis alone, but I mean the world at large, because, as we have seen, in Paris, Brussels, Orlando, and lastly, the U.K., terrorists can strike anywhere in the world; it's a cancer that can spread anywhere in the world. However, is the world, and in particular, are Western powers, doing all they can to face this danger? This is the question that I would like to ask.

Of course if we separate out what is promoted in the media and look at actions and deeds, rather than words, we see that in the case of Syria, Western countries are not doing what needs to be done to eliminate this danger, both from Syria and from the world at large. And I would like to give you one example: On December 17, 2015, the Security Council adopted Resolution 2253, under Chapter 7, which dictates stopping the financing, arming, and facilitating of terrorists into Syria. The Vienna Group, afterwards, interpreted this resolution, that it should include closing the Turkish border and not allowing armaments and finances to cross to the terrorists. On December 18, the Security Council issued Resolution 2254, which calls for a political solution in Syria.

Now, you see that the entirety of humanity focusses on 2254, without dealing with 2253, which is a logical prerequisite for 2254, that is, for finding a political solution in Syria.

The same thing can be said about humanitarian assistance. Instead of focussing on ending the war in Syria and restoring peace and security in Syria, we see that the entire corporate media is speaking about humanitarian assistance, as if this is the issue! Syria, before this war, was able to host 2 million Iraqis and to feed itself, and to export food to 84 countries in the world. It is since the 1970s that the Syrian people have adopted the motto, "We eat from what we produce, and we wear from what we manufacture," which means that Syria does not need humanitarian help if there is peace and stability, and if the Syrian people are able to develop their crops and attend to their factories.

Today we hear a lot of talk from the Western alliance about "containing" ISIS, "limiting" ISIS; and lastly, you all heard the speech of CIA Director John Brennan, who said that we did not succeed even in limiting the influence of ISIS. Why? Because there is no real desire and wish, really, to get rid of ISIS. There were two elements: The Russian government had called on Western countries to join efforts to defeat ISIS both in Syria and Iraq, and the agreement in Vienna was that the Turkish borders should be closed. Neither of these two elements received a positive response from the United States or the Western powers. The question is, why?—if there is a real will to fight ISIS.

The other question is, that we in Syria feel that what is needed is a real will in the international community to fight terrorism and to build real bridges. When I say "real bridges," I mean, on an equal basis, on a basis of parity. The problem with promoting "democracy"—in quotation marks—in our part of the world, is that Western countries believe that liberal democracy is the only issue, or the only copy, or the only formula that should be applied to our countries. And this is not true, because we all have different cultures.

We have different identities, we have different habits, we have different ways of life, and I can give an example: China, India, the Persian culture, Arab culture have contributed a great deal to the world, but on a *human* basis, and on a basis of parity. In fact, here I would like to make an important point, that the Western world believes in opening markets to the entire world, but only to export its own goods! But *not* to allow other countries to export to the West, on an equal basis. And every day they invent different formulas in order not to allow equal treatment—tariff constraints and other constraints.

Intellectual Silk Road

The same thing applies to politics. The concepts, values, and ideas, coming from the West should be respected and implemented in our countries, but there is no other road that takes our culture, and our values and our ethics to the West. If we need to create a world for all, if we need to create a peaceful world, if we need to create a prosperous world for all, we need to create a conceptual, intellectual concept of one world; we need to create a conceptual concept of a Silk Road. Not only an actual Silk Road, but an *intellectual* Silk Road. All of you know that Aleppo and Syria were extremely crucial in the ancient Silk Road that connected Asia to Europe. Syria and the Syrian people will be more than happy to be very active also in a New Silk Road and in a political, social, intellectual Silk Road that connects Asia to the West, that connects Eurasia to the West.

The other byproduct of this war on our countries, and the other byproduct of promoting only Western exceptionalism in our country, is the distortion of the image of Islam in Western eyes. Islam, like any other religion, is a religion of love, a religion of humanity. We, as Muslims, were hardly ever, if ever, addressed in our Quran as Muslims. We are addressed as "ye human beings": We are part of the human community. And therefore, those who kill in the name of Islam, those who destroy in the name of Islam, are not Muslims at all. They have nothing to do with Islam.

We have to address the concept that the terrorists are promoting, and the lack of dialogue that the corporate media are causing, if we want to create a truly prosperous Silk Road, not only physical, but also intellectual, social, and political. And here, I would like to conclude by thanking Russia and China, who right from the beginning of the war on Syria, took four vetoes against Western attempts to try to strike Syria militarily. And Russia, and China, and Iran, continue to support the Syrian people, to try to find a political solution.

In brief, what I would like to say here is that, in order to build these Silk Roads, we have to deal with each other on an equal basis, on an equal *human* basis, and dealing otherwise, as superior and inferior, as white and black, as important and less important, is producing extremism, is producing racism which is striking not only in Syria, but in Brussels, in Paris, in Orlando, and last of all in the U.K. Thus, it is in the interests of humanity to think as human beings, to think of the world as truly a human village, where people live equally, and have mutual respect for each other, and deal on the basis of parity.

But this requires a huge change in the mindset of the West, that probably requires another conference, to speak not only about the very important idea launched by China, of building a Silk Road, but to speak about the intellectual, social, and political Silk Road, that thinks and deals with all of us, as human, as brothers and sisters, rather than as superior and inferior. Thus, we can build a new world, and one world, and a much better world than the one we live in. We have an obligation to our grandchildren, wherever they are born, to leave them a better world than this one in which we live now.

Thank you very much.

Discussion with Dr. Shaaban

Directly after the video, Dr. Shaaban appeared live on Skype, and received a standing ovation from the audience of the conference. She answered several questions and demonstrated the double standard of the sanctions and the war on Syria. A German Arabist in the audience asked for her view of the German policy against Syria. Dr. Shaaban recounted how shocked the whole of Syria had been to hear a German parliamentarian, coming out of a vote to send uninvited German troops to Syria, saying that he did not know anything about the issue.

Helga Zepp-LaRouche took the microphone and expressed her appreciation for Dr. Shaaban's presentation, and vowed to spread the word about what is really going on in Syria.

PROJECT PHOENIX
Video: The Reconstruction of Aleppo

Project Phoenix was initiated by the Schiller Institute and Swedish architect Greger Ahlberg to plan the rebuilding of Syria from the ashes. This video on the reconstruction of Aleppo was produced by a Schiller Institute team, assisted by a group of Syrian archaeologists and architects who are living in Germany as refugees.

The video begins by showing what the city of Aleppo looked like before the war, and what it looks like now, after the destruction of war. Aleppo, the crossroads of the ancient Silk Road, has risen and fallen many times, and will rise again like a Phoenix.

In November 2015, a Schiller Institute delegation and the Syrian-Swedish Committee for Democracy travelled to Damascus to present Project Phoenix. In the meantime, developments anticipated by the institute, such as the institutionalization of the BRICS organization and the One Belt, One Road policy, had materialized.

Project Phoenix consists of two major sections: (1) How to finance reconstruction, and (2) How Syria can benefit from connecting to the New Silk Road.

Reconstruction must be financed by a combination of national (Hamiltonian) credit and foreign export financing and direct investments. Resources should be allocated for emergency housing programs, and rebuilding schools, hospitals, and other services for millions of refugees and the population which has lost them through the war.

At the same time, industries and agricultural facilities destroyed by the war must be rebuilt. Among these, pharmaceutical and petrochemical industries are of strategic importance. The Syrian transport system must be upgraded and expanded to connect the domestic network to transcontinental routes from the "Five Seas," as developed in the "Five Seas Strategy" (Mediterranean, Indian Ocean, Red Sea, Caspian Sea, and Black Sea) that President Bashar al-Assad presented in 2009, before the war broke out.

The New Silk Road involves two development corridors, one East-West and the other North-South, which will bring long-term vitality and growth to the ancient crossroads of Syria. The video presents maps showing all connections from Syria to the three continents and the Five Seas. In this new network of corridors for transport and development, Syria will resume—in the New Silk Road—its historic pivotal role in the old. All of these routes will intersect in Aleppo, Syria's largest city, as it has been for hundreds of years.

Before the war, Syria was not a rich country, but it had a relatively good living standard and free education and health care systems. The city of Aleppo hosted 30-40% of Syrian manufacturing capability. Some 10 kilometers north of Aleppo is the Sheikh Najar industrial city, whose construction began in 2000, equipped with advanced equipment and facilities. Both this city and Aleppo have been destroyed. The development process must be resumed, and continued in other parts of the country.

Aleppo is a beautiful city of history and art; it must be restored to its true character as a center for universal culture and civilization. It must become the world capital for the dialogue of civilizations!

TALAL MOUALLA

Towards a New, Modern Cultural Approach

Talal Moualla is on the board of trustees of the Syria Trust for Development, and is executive director of the Ministry of Culture's Syrian Cultural Heritage Transformation Project. He titled his address, "Repositioning of the Cultural Variable: Towards a New, Modern Cultural Approach." He spoke in Arabic, with simultaneous translation by panel moderator Hussein Askary.

Having come directly from Syria, Talal Moualla described the war in Syria as being an attack on its heritage and culture, as well as on its people and state. But the target is not only Syria, he said, as there is a world heritage with roots in our civilization.

He said, "My own studio was burned down by the terrorists with one hundred paintings in it. I am not worried about these as much as I am worried about the overall cultural heritage of the country, and its position throughout history as a producer of culture and civilization. I have been working for the Syria Trust for Development and the Culture Ministry to find ways to recover and restore the soul of the Syrian people. We are doing this in cooperation with civil society organizations and individuals, collecting their stories—both their folklore stories and new ones that they have created during the war.

"We are using creativity and beauty to encounter the bestiality of the enemy. We have had a terrible mass exodus of intellectuals from the country. The intellectuals have a very important role in working with the people and government institutions to restore the Syrian character, soul, and heritage."

He invited everyone to meet again in Damascus.

FOUAD AL-GHAFFARI

Confronting the Aggressor with Hope for the Future

Fouad Al-Ghaffari is chairman of the Advisory Office for Coordination with the BRICS, Yemen.

In a video sent to the conference, Fouad Al-Ghaffari regretted that he was not able to participate in person. He enumerated the achievements of his office in promoting "a clear vision for a creative and productive credit system and for building a future for the nation along the New Silk Road."

These achievements included publishing and distributing thousands of copies of the Arabic version of

the *EIR* special report, *The New Silk Road Becomes the World Land-Bridge*, launching it through a conference sponsored by the Ministry of Finance, and organizing weekly public readings of the report, among others.

All of these accomplishments were achieved in a record time of four months, under the worst military attack in the history of the nation. This, he said, was made possible by the dedication and resilience of the young women and men in the Advisory Office, "who confronted the aggressors by creating hope for the future, and broke with the conventional methods of thinking."

BEREKET SIMON

Ethiopia's Economic Development in Context: the Silk Roads and Africa

Bereket Simon is Chairman of the Commercial Bank of Ethiopia and Adviser to Prime Minister Hailemariam Desalegn. He titled his address, "On the Importance of the Economic Development of Ethiopia in the context of the New Silk Road, the Maritime Silk Road, and the Greater African Region."

Mrs. Helga Zepp-LaRouche, representatives of governments and different institutions,

Dear Friends,

Ladies and Gentlemen,

It is an honor and a pleasure to be here in Berlin. First of all I would like to thank the Schiller Institute for inviting me to speak on a broad topical subject, the importance of the economic development of Ethiopia in the context of the New Silk Road, the Maritime Silk Road and the greater African region.

The term "Silk Road" refers to an ancient trade route, but my interest obviously lies in highlighting the significance of its present incarnation within the current global context. By all accounts, the old Silk Road played a vital role as a well-traversed trade route that stretched outwards from China to the Middle East, even to the shores of the Horn of Africa. This, I believe, was borne out by the history of the old Silk Road, which connected China with much of the rest of the known world.

Like its predecessor, the New Silk Road will radiate from China and straddle a vast swathe of the globe, opening up opportunities for an unprecedented level of trans-boundary exchange of goods and services. I strongly believe that the New Silk Road will not only boost the trade volume of emerging countries, but will also broaden their economic interaction.

However, in the context of changing variables of globalization, countries—especially like ours from the developing world—need to sharpen their competitive edge to fully benefit from the kind of interconnectivity that the New Silk Road brings.

It bears keeping in mind that sharpening one's trade competitiveness is tied to building a strong economy, which again relies on the ability of these countries to design and implement correct home-grown policies and strategies—as the crucial ingredient of development cannot simply be imported or dictated from abroad.

It is evident that the problem with most countries on our continent is not the lack of resources per se. The biggest challenge lies in weak capacity to design and sustainably implement such policies and strategies, without which no emerging country can effectively utilize the opportunities global connectivity offers, mitigate the adverse effects, and tap into the promising benefits of the modern Silk Road.

Hence, lest our continent miss out on the current wave of late development, the present generation of African policymakers needs to bury the legacy of dependency on foreign aid, even though external assistance, when properly sequenced and allocated, has been useful. Instead, African leaders would—if they properly mobilize domestic resources and thrive to catch up with mid-income, industrialized economies—play a commensurate role in the global economy.

Ethiopia's Course

Dear Friends, after having said this much, taking Africa in general as an entry point, I shall now return to my own country, about which I know a thing or two.

I trust that some of you are aware that Ethiopia was once home to a glorious ancient civilization, survived by at least two enduring and interdependent state and religious institutions. The records of the ancient past attest to Ethiopia's long and fascinating history of interaction with the great Mediterranean, Indian, and possibly Chinese civilizations.

However, in the last few hundred years in general and the last half of the 20th Century in particular, Ethiopia entered into a prolonged period of stagnation, followed by a steep decline that continued right up to the dawn of the modern era. The failure of successive regimes to accommodate diversity, and their inability to meet the aspirations of the peoples of Ethiopia, significantly contributed to its downward spiral.

Although, throughout these centuries, Ethiopia managed to retain and defend its independence from foreign aggression, yet the country missed out on the great global transformation. As the rest of Ethiopia's historical peer states underwent significant changes, our country remained mired in stagnation characterized by recurrent drought, famine, and internal strife.

The cumulative effects of centuries of social and economic stagnation sadly worsened to the point of state failure during the long seventeen years of military rule that ravaged the country from year 1974 to 1991. The command economic system pursued by the military junta, combined with its repressive policy against nationalist demands for political autonomy, left the country in shambles.

Hence, after the fall of the military state in 1991, the successor coalition government of the Ethiopian People's Revolutionary Democratic Front (EPRDF) saw peace and reconciliation as its first order of business.

With a sense of urgency, the leadership exerted enormous effort and succeeded in stabilizing the polarized political landscape of post-conflict Ethiopia by a radical institutional design of governance. The upshot, I am proud to say, is the present inclusive constitutional federal system that provides for all basic individual and group democratic rights.

Once lasting peace had been secured, the leadership turned its attention to the equally pressing task of dismantling the inherited command economy and the institutional barriers it had created. This prompt measure released the market from counterproductive state interference and even spurred a modest GDP growth of around 5% for the first twelve years. But, to the post-military regime Ethiopian leadership, led by the late Prime Minister Meles Zenawi, even a higher percentage of single-digit growth was inadequate to turn around this country with an alarming index of population growth.

Against Neoliberal Prescriptions

The big question, therefore, that the leadership had to squarely address in those years was, by what policies and strategy could it be possible to accelerate growth in a war-torn, underdeveloped country with a fledgling market economy and a tiny private sector? Nonetheless, at this point in history the developing world had not been granted sufficient space to formulate and implement policies other than those prescribed by the Washington consensus. However, Ethiopia from the outset defied such policy prescriptions based on the conventional wisdom of "one size fits all" and opted to formulate its own policy based on the objective reality of the country.

Indeed, we in Ethiopia had, from the outset, defined poverty as our biggest enemy with which no compromise is possible. It was our firm conviction, too, that in a country like ours, where the market and the private sector are at their rudimentary stage of development, no serious developmental undertaking that addresses this core existential issue would succeed without the proper role of the state. It is based on this conviction that, throughout the last 25 years, we committed to promoting and defending our national economic development path, which gives the state a prominent role in influencing the speed and direction of Ethiopia's development. Yet, the path we have chosen allows for both the public sector and the market to play a complementary role in terms of generating national wealth marked by relative equitable distribution.

Development Led by Agriculture

Against the misgivings of neoliberal establishments, our initial answer to the daunting task of fighting poverty lay in the state-directed, agriculture-led development policy and strategy aimed at poverty reduction. This is because agriculture, and specifically that of the small-holding farmers, is the backbone of our economy on which depends the livelihood of the overwhelming majority of our people.

Granted, our second Growth and Transformation Plan aims to lay the foundation for an accelerated economic transition led by the manufacturing sector, but we still continue to invest in small-holding agriculture as the main growth driver of our economy. There are times when severe drought occasionally reduces our agricultural output, as it did in 2004 and in this last harvest season; we have managed, however, to raise our agricultural production from somewhere around 7.5 million metric tons to over 30 million metric tons in 2014.

Increased production has enabled our nation to cope with the devastation of the 2015 El Nin@afo-induced drought that left millions of Ethiopians in need of emergency food assistance. The fact that no drought-related death occurred despite the severity of crop failure, I believe, speaks to the capacity and resilience of our agricultural economy to absorb natural disasters.

Climate change is no doubt one of the biggest challenges of our planet. That is why only a concerted global response can mitigate the terrible consequences of climate change, particularly for countries dependent on agriculture. To do our part, we have already put in place a Climate-Resilient Green Economic Program, which is bound to make our country less vulnerable to the vagaries of climate change. We are proud that with every passing year millions of Ethiopian farming households are investing their energy in water and soil conservation projects across the country. This had been one of the main reasons that Ethiopia was able to withstand the effects of the El Nin@afo induced current drought.

It is not by accident that Ethiopia today is rated as one of the fastest and most equitably growing economies in Africa. Ethiopia has allocated 70% of its budget for pro-poor programs, such as education, health, agriculture, and food security, which helped it to register an average economic growth rate of 10.6% over the last 13 years.

However, we are the first to caution ourselves against the danger of falling into complacency by forgetting that such a high rate of growth is an index of a weak starting base. In any event, our tiger rate of development still gives us much hope and confidence in our ability to attain the goals envisioned in our ambitious second Growth and Transformation Plan.

Towards Rapid Industrial Development

While we have given agriculture the top-most priority in the last decade, Ethiopia is gearing itself towards a rapid industrial development as well. To this effect, it has initiated a massive micro and small enterprises development program, together with the expansion of medium and heavy industries. We have heavily invested in micro and small-scale enterprises with high social return in the form of reduction of unemployment. Like many developing nations where the number of the young constitutes the majority, creating job and employment opportunities and gender empowerment are very critical to Ethiopia.

Investing in the development of micro and small enterprises, as a launching base for industrial development, has not only alleviated poverty to an appreciable degree; it has also given rise to a sizable middle class and business community with sufficient capital to invest in the growing manufacturing and service sector of Ethiopia.

Social development is equally important if Ethiopia is to continue with the pace of development that it has initiated. Hence, today, over 28 million citizens are attending school in one grade cycle or another. This is the equivalent of educating the entire demography of the 20 African countries having less than four million population.

In addition to this, with our flagship primary health-care program, we have deployed close to 40,000 health extension workers across the country during the last decade. Thus, Ethiopia has managed to reduce the child mortality rate by close to 30% in the past five years alone. The proportion of people living in abject poverty has declined by nearly 35% in the last fourteen years. As a result, life expectancy at birth has risen from 45 in 1991 to 64 years in 2015. These results, I believe, are a testament to the effectiveness of the pro-poor development policies and strategies that the Ethiopian developmental state, previously led by the late Prime Minister Meles Zenawi, has achieved.

In line with this, Ethiopia has embarked on nurturing the private sector as the engine of our industrial development. A glance at the visible renovation of our cities, a function of the urban renewal program led by the newly created private sector, suffices to demonstrate the important role Ethiopian entrepreneurs play in our overall development today. Without this pivotal role by the private sector, the current rapid economic growth would have remained a pipe dream.

Large Infrastructure Projects

In the age of globalization, increased private sector investment, which is necessary for a competitive economy, obviously depends on the availability and expansion of physical infrastructure. Today most of the major mega-projects in Africa are found in Ethiopia. The Grand Ethiopian Renaissance Dam (GERD), which is one of the largest in Africa, will produce 6,000 megawatts of electric power at completion, and the national railway line project, covering the entire north-south and east-west axes of the country, are only two good examples in this respect. The fact that Ethiopia has started graduating around 70,000 students in engineering and science fields every year plays a pivotal role in the development of its engineering industry.

Likewise, though fraught with difficulties, Ethiopia has cultivated a good and peaceful, neighborly relationship with most of the countries in the Horn. The fact that Ethiopia has initiated some infrastructural programs with Kenya, Djibouti, Sudan, and the South Sudan is expected to have a much broader impact in terms of sustaining the cooperative spirit toward a better regional integration.

One cannot, however, underestimate the difficulties of sustaining diplomatic and trade relations in the Horn of Africa, a region threatened by international terrorism. I believe this represents one of the most serious challenges that need to be overcome in order to build this new economic belt through the Silk Road.

From the above limited facts, it can be seen that Ethiopia is indeed registering rapid change in every aspect, which is why it has become one of the preferred destination points for foreign direct investment in Africa. A trainable young workforce, a stable political system, a rapidly transforming society that contains the second largest population on the continent is, we believe, the best venue for those who would like to engage in long-term investments. Ethiopia's efforts to join the global community, in the new expanded Silk Road, are based on such thorough preparation.

One Belt, One Road

Dear Friends, Ethiopia considers China's Silk Road Economic Belt and Maritime Silk Road projects, jointly known as "One Belt and One Road," as another milestone opportunity that could contribute to Ethiopia sustaining its economic development, together with all the countries in our region. We believe, as the last decade or so has witnessed the resurgence of trade between Africa and the East, the new Silk Road would also further strengthen the mutual benefits of expanded trade between nations. This will also apply to the relationship between Ethiopia and its traditional partners. The fact that not only development assistance, but also foreign direct investment from Europe and the United States had been instrumental in the rapid economic development of the country, is another proof that mutually beneficial relations could bring about a guaranteed positive outcome.

Finally, I would like to conclude by saying that, since the adoption of a new economic direction 25 years ago, we have come a long way. We were able to achieve double-digit economic growth for over a decade, build important governance institutions, significantly increase our contribution to regional and continental peace and stability, and put in place major infrastructure networks for regional integration. We are conscious that the journey ahead of us will continue to be challenging, as we have to overcome the adverse effects of climate change.

As a country, Ethiopia is determined to realize its vision of becoming a middle-income country by 2025. To this end we will strive hard to strengthen and nurture our fledgling democracy, as well as peace and regional stability. We draw inspiration from the great achievements of the last two and half decades, as we prepare ourselves to further build our country's competitiveness in the current global framework. Together with our neighbors in the region, we are determined to attain an Ethiopian, and indeed an African Renaissance which can harness the new possibilities opened by developments like the New Silk Road.

The Frontiers of Science: The New Economic Platform Based on a Fusion Economy and Man's Future in Space

ALAIN GACHET

Radar Groundwater Mapping: Turning Difficulties into Opportunities

Alain Gachet is the Chairman of Radar Technologies International, France. He titled his address, "Space Technologies Can Change the Groundwater Geopolitical Balance: Case Studies in Kenya and Iraq."

Dr. Gachet presented the WATEX (water exploration) program, which searches for underground water resources using radar mapping done from satellites. Today, when 1.1 billion human beings are without access to clean water, and water needs are growing with a growing world population, he said that science is the only way to "convert difficulties into opportunities." The water used by mankind so far is only a fraction of what is there in the deep underground—the real source of water.

WATEX got into action in the 2004 drought in Sudan and found water at a depth of 80 meters. Once drilling was done, the water was sufficient to supply 33 million people and make the trucking of water, at a cost of $500 million, superfluous.

During the 2011 drought in northern Kenya, WATEX found a water basin half the size of Belgium, containing 200 billion cubic meters of water. By 2014, the Hell created by the drought in northern Kenya had been turned into paradise: The former drought zone was producing an abundance of vegetables from newly created arable land.

The WATEX approach is to make use of the characteristics of soil wetness and soil roughness that one can determine with space-based radar, and a particular difference between water and oil. This method was also used in Iraq, and abundant underground water resources were found in the country's eastern regions. The same could be done for Syria and other countries with large arid zones.

There was applause when Gachet showed a short video of African children refreshing themselves joyfully at a new water well and fountain—it was the first clean water they had experienced in their young lives.

RAINER SANDAU

Towards a New Era of International Space Cooperation

Rainer Sandau of Germany is Technical Director, Satellite and Space Applications, of the International Academy of Astronautics.

Dr. Sandau presented the work of his organization, the International Academy of Astronautics (IAA), from its founding in 1960. The IAA, which promotes interchange among researchers, technology developers, and astronauts internationally, has won 1,200 members for its effort to alert policy makers to the necessity of space exploration. Among the IAA regional secretaries is one in Syria, who has made important contributions to this cause.

When the International Space Station was first put into orbit around Earth, there were eight space agencies supporting the program. Since then, many new agencies have been created. There are 40 of them now, and the IAA has brought many of their leaders together at international summits—most recently in 2010, 2014, and 2015—under its motto, "Together to Space to Enrich All on Earth."

ADELINE DJEUTIE

Nuclear Energy in Developing Countries

The third presentation in this panel was by Adeline Djeutie (Cameroon), who has worked with the International Atomic Energy Agency and is now an independent consultant in Vienna, in areas related to IAEA work. Her prepared statement follows.

Adeline Djeutie, independent consultant, former programme management officer at the International Atomic Energy Agency, Division for Africa, Technical Cooperation, entitled her presentation: "Sustaining Energy Development in Developing and Emerging Countries: What Role Could Nuclear Energy Play?"

Energy plays a critical role in economic and social development. In fact, there is no development or poverty alleviation possible without a reliable and sustainable supply of energy. Energy contributes to improving social conditions (health, education, food and decent living) and economic development (private sector development, investment, employment, industrialisation, and innovation). Yet, many developing countries are still not able to meet the energy demand needs placed on them, to incubate the necessary conditions that could trigger effective development and alleviate poverty. 1.4 billion people still lack access to energy, most of them in developing countries. According to the United Nations world population growth forecast, population will increase from 6.7 billion in 2011 to 8.7 billion by 2035, increasing substantially the demand on energy. Over 70% of that increase of demand is expected from developing countries led by China and India.

In regions like Africa, the energy poverty does not reflect the existing natural resources potential in many countries. In fact, Africa is endowed with various natural resources (oil, gas, coal, sun, water, wind, and uranium, for example) that could sufficiently fill the current and expected energy demand gap if some bottlenecks were overcome and adequate measures were taken.

As for specific examples, it is indeed a paradox that in the Democratic Republic of Congo, only 9% of the population has access to electricity, whereas the country has a huge hydropower potential[1]. Nigeria, although one of the top oil producer countries in the world and member of OPEC, can supply electricity to only 55.6% of its population. Niger and Namibia are the 4th and 5th leading world producers of uranium, but only 14.4% and 47.3 % of their respective populations have access to electricity[2].

Access to traditional and renewable sources of energy has been limited, so far, due to several factors such as political instability, lack of investment funds, heavy domestic regulatory policies, technological barriers, small market size, and weak transmission connections within countries and with neighbouring countries.

Climate change and recent environmental disorders have been attributed to the retaliation of both natural and social systems to unsustainable use of limited natural resources and destruction of our ecosystem over the past centuries. We have witnessed some devastating environmental catastrophes recently in all continents, and developing countries have been most vulnerable to their long term adverse effects, which poses an additional challenge to their national development agendas. There has been an international clamour to urgently curb greenhouse gas emission (GHG) trends, and calls for greening the economy have reached a point of no return.

Renewable energy is promoted as a source of alternative clean energies. There are several financial and investment incentives for energy development policies from traditional donors and investors, that preferentially support energy from sources that are abundant and infinite like wind, solar, geothermal, and to some

extent, water. Nuclear power, that had its glorious years until the middle of the 1980s, seems to be portrayed as **obsolete,** and therefore discarded as a widespread viable option, from major energy policy and development discussions at the international level.

The End of Nuclear Energy Era?

Yet nuclear power has so far proven to be a clean and reliable source of energy. There were about 435 nuclear reactors in operation in the world by the end of 2014[3], most of them in the U.S.A. (99), France (58), Japan (48), Russia (34), China (23), Republic of Korea (23) and India (21)[4]. Nuclear power has long contributed to the development of the industrialised countries. The Fukushima-Daiichi accident in 2011 has rightly sparked some hot debates and strong mobilisations at various levels, to phase out nuclear power programmes that are considered too risky and unsafe. The popular opinion of nuclear opponents still considers that energy salvation should come from innovation and technological progress in other renewable sources. But the unknown factor is whether the cost and capacities of other renewable sources could effectively replace nuclear in the respective national energy mixes, and also, if so, will the population be willing to bear the necessary cost?

In the meantime, despite some major slowdown in the industry since the Fukushima-Daiichi accident, and strong negative public perceptions about nuclear power especially in Europe, the reality is that many countries still rely on this source to ensure a stable and affordable supply of energy for their populations. Based on a study conducted by the IAEA, nuclear electricity still holds a big share in the energy portfolio of the so called 34 nuclear power countries. Between 1985 and 2014, nuclear electricity's share accounted for 76.9% in France, 47.5% in Belgium, 30.4 % in Japan, 19.5% in the United States of America and 15.8% in Germany[5]. This share is also very important in Central European countries (Slovakia—56.9%, Hungary—53.6%, Ukraine—49.4%, Slovenia—37.1%, Czech Republic—35.9%, Bulgaria—33.6%, Armenia—30.7%), and varies for the other nuclear power countries.

1. Africa Energy Outlook 2014, IEA
2. http://data.worldbank.org/indicator/EG.ELC.ACCS.ZS

3. http://www-pub.iaea.org/books/IAEABooks/10903/Nuclear-Power-Reactors-in-the-World-2015-Edition
4. Same as above.
5. Same as above

At the same time, traditional nuclear power countries like Russia, Japan, the U.S.A., and France are expanding their nuclear capacity in order to increase the share of nuclear electricity, but the biggest shift is now seen in such emerging countries as India, China, Pakistan, U.A.E., and Turkey, which aim to expand energy production to support their fast growing economies and populations. These new trends trigger some prospects for analysis that could be further explored for other less developed countries' business models. In fact, the strong interest of emerging countries in developing or expanding their nuclear power programs, indicates the potential that lies in this source of energy, beyond its known risks. Such potential is worth further exploring, without any taboo or prejudgement.

Climate Change, Development, and the Role of Nuclear Power

After so many years of international development efforts, developing countries, along with the development-agency communities, have failed to implement energy policies that are consistent with the real needs, and commensurate with the challenges faced by these countries. With so many development priorities, developing countries have a lot on their plates, which makes it hard to keep up with the ever-changing international agenda. Climate change agreements are adding substantial challenges to these countries; thus their reluctance to strongly commit to and embrace the global effort to combat climate change. As regards energy, many, if not all of these countries are heavily dependent on international finance to support domestic energy infrastructure. Now such financial supports are offered to clean development technologies, except for nuclear. Looking at the development patterns of rich countries: almost all, if not all, at some point in their development, had to embark on nuclear power. The question to ask nowadays is whether socio-economic development is possible without nuclear power, taking into consideration current development indicators and energy demand forecasts, and comparing other successful development models.

It is indeed striking to see, from the list of nuclear power countries, that emerging countries in Asia and Central Europe are taking the lead in nuclear power development investments, and their share is expected to grow steadily over the coming decades. It is obvious that as the standards of living and levels of development of some countries increase, so does the demand for quality in terms of water, air, energy, food and other commodities. Full and affordable energy supply remains the concern of developing countries for the time-being.

Taking into consideration that nuclear is a mature technology, for which particular safety requirements should be put in place, innovation and technological development could also contribute to mitigate some safety risks, bearing in mind that no zero-risk scenario exists in any technological breakthrough. Further considerations of the role of nuclear in development will be discussed during the session.

In her oral presentation and discussion, Adeline Djeutie said that there is an urgent need for a change of paradigm, to create a world free of fear, of need, and of disease, with freedom to develop energy as a key resource for economic and social life. She reported that in many meetings, when she said she was in the nuclear business, discussion partners distanced themselves, influenced by the ignorance and disinformation created by mass media campaigns, especially after the Fukushima accident five years ago. But the truth is that energy supplies globally, particularly in many Afrcan countries, do not measure up to the actual energy needs, which will increase further with the growing world population. There are African countries rich in uranium sources, but the population there mostly has no access to energy supplies. Congo has abundant water sources but no hydropower to supply its population. The fast-growing economies in southeast Asia show that with nuclear power, rapid development is possible, and there are not enough nuclear power plants in the world yet: only 405 of them are in operation now. More nuclear power is also the way to improve the world climate, but after Fukushima, the alleged end of nuclear power was proclaimed, launching a policy of fear. That has to be reversed, and Africa already has a significant skilled workforce to change policiy, although now it is living and working in the diaspora outside of Africa.

The Positive Historical Traditions and Renaissance Periods Linking Europe to China, to Russia, to America, and to the Arab World

GIAN MARCO SANNA

A Window to a New World

Gian Marco Sanna is a violinist, and founder and artistic director of the Geminiani Project, a string ensemble based in London, which plays at A=432.

(The Geminiani Project performed three musical pieces at the Dialogue of Culture concert on Saturday night.)

Gian Marco Sanna explained that he first heard about tuning to A=432 on the internet a few years ago, which was a window to a new universe. The Berlin Philharmonic is now still playing at A=446. He read about experiments on soldiers run by Goebbles, Hitler's propaganda minister, which showed that higher tuning increased the heart rate, and the aggressivity of the soldiers. Sanna decided to use this power for the good. In 2012, on the 250th anniversary of the Italian composer Geminiani, who worked in London, Sanna decided to found a string ensemble.

He experienced wonderful things after he tuned his 18th Century violin down to A=432. The "wolf" dissonant effect disappeared, the sound was more balanced, and sweeter. Upon reflection, he understood

that the "screaming" quality of his previous violin, and viola, were not due to the instruments, but their tuning.

From then on, he only played at A=432, which meant he had to refuse jobs. He learned that specific frequencies were used in other situations, such as making mechanical parts more flexible, to create certain effects in water.

But the best way to hear the difference the Verdi tuning makes, is to hear the quality of the performances. He told of the reaction of one family that attended classical concerts every week. After hearing Sanna's ensemble, they said that they had never heard this quality of sound. "What did you do?"

Sanna said that he can't see himself doing anything else, and this is why he is at the conference.

Benjamin Lylloff, who had organized the concert Saturday night, said that the warm sound changed people, and referred to the Schiller Institute's campaign 20 years ago for the Verdi tuning.

Sanna said that he had seen headlines at that time about Renata Tebaldi bringing a suit against the opera house because they didn't play at Verdi tuning, but he didn't understand it at that time. But, now is the right moment.

HUSSEIN ASKARY

The Beauty of the Islamic Renaissance—The Elephant Clock

EIR's Southwest Asia specialist and Arabic editor, Hussein Askary, delivered this presentation at the June 25-26 Schiller Insitute conference on June 26.

When you say the word "Islamic" nowadays, it triggers associations with terrorism, extremism, and fundamentalism. Many of these associations have a certain basis in reality, but that reality is almost completely an artificial construction of political, strategic, and intelligence institutions that intend to keep the world divided and concurred. Militant Islam is a relatively modern phenomenon and became known when the United States, Britain, and Saudi Arabia financed, armed and trained the so-called Mujahideen in Afghanistan to fight against the Soviet army.

But the Muslim nations and societies themselves are also partly to blame for neglecting the great aspects of scientific, philosophical, and artistic heritage of the Islamic culture. We often hear nostalgic statements and speeches full of empty pride about "the great achievements of Islam." But we seldom see studies and lively discussions on the details of how, when, and who created those great achievements. Everywhere you go in

the Arab world, you see Ibn Sina Hospital or Ibn Sina School, Al-Kindi Hospital or Al-Kindi School, Arrazi Hospital or Arrazi School. But how many Arabs or Muslims today really know what those scientific and philosophical giants achieved or how they thought? And also in what atmosphere they worked and thought?

It is of course, not possible to sum up the answers for these questions, because the homework has not been done to answer them. What I want to do here is to provoke some thoughts, and urge people to do this homework, because it is urgent now, in light of the terrible things being done in the name of Islam, and in light of the terrible things being done to Muslim societies and the other minorities living within them.

Now, as I have written and presented in various occasions, the Islamic Renaissance, whose Golden Age extended from the late 8th Century into the end of the 13th Century, was not simply Islamic. It was not simply Arab, although Arabic was the *lingua franca* of that time from the borders of China in the East to northern Spain in the West. I may dare to say that the Islamic Renaissance was not a religious phenomenon, although it was based on the teachings of Islam which urged the believers to "seek knowledge from the cradle to the grave." The Islamic Renaissance was rather a cultural phenomenon, a unique one, because it was a synthesis of Arabic, Persian, Greek, Egyptian, Indian, Chinese and other cultures. In Baghdad in the 9th Century you had Muslim, Christian, and Jewish scientists and translators in the House of Wisdom working without prejudice, to translate and verify Greek, Indian, Chinese, Persian, and all kinds of scientific and philosophical manuscripts. The same thing was going on in Cordoba in Andalusia, Spain.

In order to give a metaphorical image of this beautiful synthesis, I chose this image of the elephant clock, a piece of mechanical and artistic work done by Badi-Uzzaman al-Jazari, who lived between 1136-1206 in the Al-Jazira area northeast of modern Syria. Al-Jazira means "the island," but here it refers to the land between the Tigris and Euphrates. Hence his name, Al-Jazari. Al-Jazari was a true polymath: a mathematician, artist, artisan, musician, and mechanical engineer. His most known book is "The Book of Knowledge of Ingenious Mechanical Devices." Actually the original Arabic title says something like "Combining science with beneficial work in mechanics." In this book, he describes about 100 mechanical inventions he had made and how they can be reconstructed or built. He made miniature paintings with instructions on how to build these mechanical works. Now, what is interesting for me and for you is not the mechanics themselves, but the method of thinking, which is a great metaphor for the true dialog of cultures, of what al-Jazari had in mind, and what he understood to be the message of Islam.

But let's take a look at one of his most known inventions, the mechanical "Elephant Clock."

For an explanation of how the clock works, see this video! https://www.youtube.com/watch?v=doYPp-gaJ0o

Al-Jazari consciously put a phoenix bird on top, which represents the ancient Egyptian mythological deity Bennu, and is also part of Greek culture. As you may know, Egyptian and Greek were almost one culture for certain important periods, as we understand from Plato's dialogues, and later collaboration between Archimedes and Eratosthenes, the Dean of the Library of Alexandria. The serpents or dragons symbolize China, the elephant and the deity with the cymbal refer to India, the architecture and furniture are Persian and Arabian, and the water technique is a reference to Greece.

This work, in a very beautiful and efficient way, reflects and encapsulates the whole idea of the beauty of the Islamic culture, and the spirit of the diversity in the oneness that was dominant at the time. The Holy Quran states: "O mankind, indeed We created you from one male and one female, and made you into peoples and tribes that you may know one another. Indeed, the most noble of you in the eyes of Allah are the most righteous ones."

Can we revive that spirit today? This is the big question.

Final Discussion Session

This is the final conference discussion, which took place at the end of the conference, with the participation of Lyndon LaRouche and Helga Zepp-LaRouche, the speakers from the scientific panel IV, and Hussein Askary.

This discussion session was opened with the following remarks by Helga Zepp-LaRouche:

Europe is in turmoil. After the Brexit vote, Great Britain and Europe are in shock. In Beijing, Putin and Xi signed 30 major deals, cementing their alliance. Between now and the summit meeting in Vladivostok in September, a lot will change. We have to make sure that our idea that Europe must join the Silk Road will have the maximum impact, to let people know that the alternative exists. A dialogue of cultures is the most effective means we have, like the concert last night. Use the power of classical culture to open the hearts and minds. Humans have the potential to perfect themselves. Schiller said that a great moment found a little people. Political change can only be brought about through ennoblement of the individual. I have been dedicated to that idea, and that is why I founded the Schiller Institute.

Discussion

Leonidas Chrysanthopoulos, to nuclear consultant Adeline Djeutie: I am against nuclear power because of Chernobyl. Why not use renewable energy?

Djeutie: No technology is without risk. This can only be overcome by research. We have to balance advantages and risks. The scientific community has learned from the nuclear accidents. Renewables can't be afforded by developing countries, and renewables can't cover all energy needs.

Chrysanthopoulos asked Alain Gachet, who uses space radar to find water: Can you use radar to find oil?

Gachet: Water molecules are polar, and vibrate, and that is why they show up. Oil is not polar, therefore you can't discover oil with radar. But if you know where the oil deposits are, you can still figure where there is water, but it may be contaminated by the oil.

Question to Hussein: What about Islamic banking, and where is the elephant clock?

Hussein: I forgot to say that the book by Al-Jazira was printed by the University of Aleppo, before the war. There are models in Dubai, at the "1001 inventions" exhibition, and Switzerland. All of the machines in the book are constructible. Islamic banking is a good idea. The purpose of depositing money is not to get interest, but to invest in something productive. The British banking system is now trying to re-invent "Islamic bonds," but for speculative purposes.

Lyndon LaRouche: The principle of mankind's life is the characteristic of the human mind. Everything else is junk.

Question: During Modi's trip to the United States, he cozied up to Obama, and revived hostilities towards China. Is this a traitorous move, or something else?

Lyndon LaRouche: Don't worry. The essential thing is man, and the development of the human mind. Mankind is unique. What is it about the human mind that enables us to be intelligent?

Helga: It's complicated. India is not homogeneous. There are dynamic processes. Some in India still believe in geopolitics. Modi transformed India from a regional player to a world player. They are trying to be balanced, which is not necessarily bad. The 3 million

Indians in the United States can be an important force, because we have to change the United States Many people outside the United States are anti-American because they think that Hillary and Trump are like plague- and cholera. How can we get an alliance of countries to avoid World War III? India is playing hard to get, as Chas Freeman said yesterday. But the Indian president just went to China. The BRICS is a reality. The alliance between Russia, China, and India is solid.

Andrew: lecturer from Ghana: I believe that Africans need nuclear energy. Have you convinced government officials in Africa to go for nuclear? And, how will you get permission from the international community?

Adeline Djeutie: I give the governments the information to be able to assess the potential role of nuclear power. They have to be able to make a wise decision, based on responsibility for the implications.

We don't need permission from the international community. A country is sovereign, but there are dark forces. However, governments do have to abide by standards, and that is where some of the bottlenecks lie. Plus, there can be preconditions tied to outside financing.

Michael from Sweden, who has lived in Africa, asks Gachet: Kenya has eight crops a year, and the best soils, but they are using it for coffee and tea. What is the development plan for large scale food production and water development?

Gachet: You have to feed people first. Countries should not act like California, which is an example of bad management. We need new thinking, to feed humanity first, not convert agricultural lands to cash. You can't eat cash.

Helga: We have greetings from Pres. Dr. Christoph Leitl, who is part of an organization in Austria. He has repeatedly called for an African Marshall Plan. We need the New Silk Road for Southwest Asia and Africa. Go out from this conference and spread this idea.

Question: Are there any countries starting to get nuclear power in Africa?

Adeline Djeutie: On the national level, South Africa is the only nuclear country. But, then there is a growing group of about ten interested countries at different levels including Nigeria, Egypt, Kenya, and Ghana. It can take up to 15 years from the time a decision is made. There is a recent trend in which the West

African countries have a regional approach—to build one plant. It is in the feasibility stage.

Harley Schlanger, to Helga and Lyndon LaRouche: After the destruction by the British during Bush and Obama, and faced with the possibility that it will be worse with Hillary, it is understandable that some in Europe want the United States to go into isolation mode under Trump. This is not the policy of the Schiller Institute. Will you restate what needs to be done to free us from illusions?

Helga: Trump has a background associated with mafia figures like Roy Cohen, he has an FBI connection, and is unpredictable. I wouldn't want to put the nuclear button in his hands because he is so irrational.

What can Europe do now, when we are on the verge of World War III, and the danger is so real?—if the NATO summit doesn't stop pursuing the confrontation with Russia. We have a powderkeg in the South China Sea, and NATO expansion to the Russian border. The Middle East is the Balkans of this century, and if Assad is toppled there will be war with Russia.

We need a powerful demonstration of a peace movement in Europe, saying "We do not want to be part of this war." Mrs. Merkel is a poodle of Washington, saying that we have to increase the military budget, and have more participation in the military buildup.

I ask you to help make it clear that we don't want World War III. After World War II, we said never again. The German defense minister is so driven by the ambition to be chancellor, she doesn't even know what she is doing. Look at the idea that German soldiers are at the border of Russia and Lithuania, just at the time of the 75th anniversary of Operation Barbarosa. This is a deep issue for the Russians. There is no large peace movement. You have rare moments in history where you can change things. 1989 was a star hour of history, but the chance was lost, the pathway to the peace order was not taken.

Now after the Brexit, the EU is dissolving in chaos. I have no idea where markets will go on Monday. This is a period of utmost turmoil, but use every channel to say no to World War III. If Europe says that now, the United States can't do it.

Hillary is more bellicose than Bush and Obama combined, with her hatred of Russia and China. The only way is to get a clear voice from Europe now.

Demand the New Silk Road as policy. Mobilize for a Europe from the Atlantic to the Pacific, based on integration and a new paradigm.

The balance of this report is a paraphrase of the remainder of the Question & Answer session.

Helga then made a reference to Sandau, who had spoken about international space cooperation. She said we have to think of a New Paradigm for the next 100 years. Mankind has to stop thinking of war. This is what led to the Peace of Westphalia. This time, it is not just war, but annihilation. There won't be anyone to record it. That's what people block on.

Sandau: There is a dynamic of chaos, but there are also situations that can remind us of hope. Intercosmos was establish in 1966 by the Soviets, Czechs, and East Germany for a joint space project—to put up a satellite in two years. Then Prague Spring happened in 1968. There was turmoil, and Russian and East German troops entered. But the scientists overcome politics and made it happen.

The same was the case during the struggle between Argentina and the UK over the Malvinas Islands. But a joint satellite plan worked.

Science can make a better world.

During the space director summits, we wanted to bring the big and small countries together. This is an approach to a better world, if we could transfer it to other areas, that would be good.

Lyndon LaRouche: We are on the edge of thermonuclear war, I have the names of those who are planning it now. It is directed against Russia, China, and Japan. We have to be realistic, and mobilize people to come to their senses. We could induce the community to what has to be averted. We have to take the action now to prevent that war while we can.

Sander: You are right

Lyndon LaRouche: We have to discuss it more.

Hans Schultz from Denmark: We intervened during NATO leadership debates at The People's Meeting on Bornholm. They either didn't know what Prompt Global Strike was, or they didn't want to give a response.

Along with the campaign for the Verdi tuning, we need one for anti-entropic development in composition. Verdi and Brahms were the last composers. He referenced Zarlino's book on composition.

Lyndon LaRouche: The speakers here represent truth. There is a danger to mankind on a global, or less than global scale. It is immediate. We have to deal with this. We are on the edge of it now. Many don't understand it because they don't wish to. Take action now to mobilize the sentiment of the population. There is one person like me, German Foreign Minister Frank-Walter Steinmeier, who is acting to prevent going to war. Steinmeier has a crucial role.

Christina from Denmark: I was happy to be part of the choir. Join the choir.

Question: How can we protect kids who are getting polluted by the current culture. It is in the schools. They have no way to filter it out. We can try to plant a seed at home. Should we just approach the teachers?

Question: With respect to climate change, I hope you are taking the approach of Svensmark, that there is climate change all the time. He refers to the role of the Sun in climate change, and not the way Al Gore refers to climate change. What is the solution?

Question: In America, 90% of the crops are GMO's. Putin said no to GMO. Is it evil or not?

Helga: Try to get the idea of beauty as much as possibily. Use the fact that children ask, why? You can build on that. Give them a grasp of discovery, of science, and music. But without the larger paradigm shift, it doesn't mean much. We saw the power of the "dialogue of culture" concert. The Russian children were like little angels (as long as they are singing). You saw how Dr. Shaaban reacted when I brought up Palmyra, a beautiful concert in the middle of the war. This is the power of how to change the paradigm. The conductor Valery Gergiev proposed it, and they did it in 2 days. This is understood by Putin, and China. We need the great power of music. Like in post-war Germany, Furtwängler and Schlussnuss gave concerts in the rubble fields to give hope.

In 1989, the wall came down. For a short period, people became better. They demanded Classical music, the Ninth Symphony. Music can change people for the better. I am as fearful of extinction, as I am hopeful that we are on the eve of a new epoch of mankind. It is a subjective question. Can we mobilize the morale of the people? Communicate the tension of the moment, to be able to do something extraordinary.

Sandau: With respect to climate change, nature is constantly changing the climate, due to the rotation of the Earth around its axis, solar activities, and magnetic field switches. We can't prevent that. But we contribute with our own waste, and should counteract that. The good news is that in the Arctic, the possibilities of trade now exist.

Question: I was born in the bush in Madagascar, where I learned that nature is extremely powerful. But man is part of nature too. We have to integrate the world with mankind. Have to fight *along with* climate change, to help us to find solutions. Man became more intelligent after droughts. Those who didn't adapt died. But we can invent new things. Never think that the fight is against climate change, but with it.

Lyndon LaRouche: I have a modest modification, which goes with your spirit. In my experience, it can be done. With the forces we have to fight against it, we can pre-empt the defeat. People will reject what is being put before them.

Carsten from Dresden: Listen to LaRouche about what man's role is. Martin Luther King said, if you don't have something to die for, you're not fit to live. This is our source of strength, the things we know about human beings. I am proud of German astronaut Alexander Gerst, who was on the International Space Station (ISS) with Russian and Ukrainian colleagues, and was asked how they got along with each other. Their response was to hug each other. Space flight is an example for us. Man is what he can become. We have something in ourselves which is a source of strength—Classical Culture. Man is the only species that can leave the Earth. Take the challenge to discuss the bad things, make aware how we are on the edge. But inspire people to become better, to become human.

Jacques Cheminade read the conference resolution:
"Remove Sanctions against Syria and Russia to regain world peace."

The resolution was passed by acclamation by the audience.

Closing Remarks

Lyndon LaRouche: We as a people, can agree about ideas of peaceful resolution to the crisis facing us, which is essential. Send out a clarion call, spread the word. We are not looking for war. There is a solution which can enable us not to be victimized by war again.

Helga: I encourage you to join the Schiller Institute, and equally important, follow the wise words of Lyndon LaRouche.

Let's Lift the Sanctions Against Syria and Russia to Regain Peace

We, gathered on June 26, 2016 at the Schiller Institute Conference on Creating a Common Future for Mankind and a Renaissance of Classical Culture, call for an immediate lifting of the sanctions against Syria and Russia, which are nothing but an aggressive instrument of pressure and escalation towards world war from the Western powers. Such sanctions are a reflection of the geopolitical tradition of the British Empire against the principle of national sovereignty and the advantage of the other defined by the Treaty of Westphalia.

We call instead for an international conference for the reconstruction of Syria based on the "win/win" conception of China's new Silk Road, and demand that the European countries and the United States join the Chinese proposal to rebuild Syria from the destruction that their wars have brought upon the entire Middle East region.

We have, of course, first to eradicate terrorism and be inspired by the common commitment of religions, cultures and civilizations to build a better world for each and all of us. From its history of national unity based on the convergence of the best of different cultures, let Syria become a sign of beauty for the cause of world peace through our mutual development and common creativity.

Every Day Counts In Today's Showdown To Save Civilization

II. What Is Dedication?

Resolving Upward

This is an edited transcript of LaRouche PAC's weekly call-in show, June 23, with host Dave Christie of the LaRouche PAC Policy Committee from Seattle, and guest Michael G. Steger of the LaRouche PAC Policy Committee from San Francisco. Video of the entire broadcast is available at https://www.youtube.com/watch?v=jqHr0e9Ogoc

Dave Christie: Good evening. This is Dave Christie with the LaRouche PAC Policy Committee. I'll be the moderator for tonight's Thursday Fireside Chat, June 23, 2016. We have the honor of being joined by Michael Steger, from the LaRouche PAC policy committee and former candidate for U.S. Congress, having the fun to run against Nancy Pelosi.

Anyway, this is an historic moment, and I think without further ado, I'll just turn things over to Michael, to see if he has some initial comments, and then we'll open it up for a question & answer period.

Michael Steger: Hi Dave. I don't think there's a lot I need to say in the introduction because I think we can get to most of it in the questions and answers. But there's definitely a confluence of circumstances taking place that indicates that we are at the potential point to create—on a global scale—a new economic system. The collapse of the trans-Atlantic region is at a disinte-

gration point. We see it in Europe, we see in the Presidential election in the United States, and the economic disparity. You also see it in the collapse of even major countries in South America.

At the same time, you see such a coordinated juncture of developments in Eurasia, and I think that probably is best highlighted not only in the Shanghai Cooperation Organization summit that's ongoing with most nations of Eurasia participating, but also in the upcoming summit between Putin and President Xi Jinping of China this coming weekend, at which the deep-space exploration capability that Russia and China are coordinating, along with other nations like India, is on the top of the list. And this really does indicate that there's a potential, if there's a creative orientation to create a new global economic system and avert the disaster of a nuclear war.

So I think in that context, we should just open it up for questions and have some fun.

Christie: And while we're waiting for people to get on, given the situation internationally around the war danger that Mr. LaRouche has been one of the first to highlight the nature of, and given what Lyn [Lyndon La-Rouche] has pointed out in terms of the push by the British Empire towards war,— going back as far as 2011

U.S. Air Force/Senior Airman Kenny Holston

One of the fleet of U.S. Air Force stealth bomber aircraft returning to Whiteman Air Force Base, Missouri from a bombing mission at the beginning of the war against Libya.

Dr. Frank-Walter Steinmeier, SPD party leader and German Foreign Minister.

Sigmar Gabriel, Minister of Economic Affairs and Energy.

with the death of Muammar Qaddafi, he knew that the war drive was resulting from what's developing here around the push toward the new paradigm as its developing.

Michael, do you have anything more to say about the nature of the war danger?

Wolfgang Ischinger at the 50th Munich Security Conference in Munich in 2014.

The Extraterrestrial Imperative

Steger: Yes, Helga had mentioned this last week, regarding the acknowledgment of the war danger in Europe, which was significant, and this was then followed by German Foreign Minister Steinmeier's call for a change in orientation towards Russia and the sanctions. You also have the vice chancellor of Germany Sigmar Gabriel meeting with Russian President Putin next week. And there's a couple of other people—Wolfgang Ischinger who runs the Munich Security Conference supported Steinmeier, and a German diplomat to Russia, Gernot Erler— who also have endorsed Steinmeier. So there's a real political institutional fight inside Germany and inside Europe regarding the questions of war and the war danger.

The same thing is being seen in the United States: You obviously have vocal people regarding the war danger, such as Stephen Cohen. But we've even seen people like Gov. Jerry Brown, who's wrong on practically everything, but seems to be right on the dangers of nuclear war at this point.

And I would say that's even preceded by a recognition in the population. This is what underlies the revolt you see happening in the trans-Atlantic, by the population. They recognize that this system is collapsing, and its ultimate act will be nuclear war and annihilation. As the late space pioneer Krafft Ehricke said, unless we leave the confines of planet Earth,— given the level of industry, the level of development taking place in the 20th Century, the *only* way that mankind can find a perpetual state of collaboration and development is to leave the confines of Earth. He said: I find it an abysmal condition that mankind will be stuck on the planet with the potential to annihilate itself. And that the only way to overcome that challenge is really to go to an extraterrestrial development program.

And that's why it's so significant that what Russia and China are embarking upon is not simply challeng-

Russian President Vladimir Putin and Xi Jinping, President of the People's Republic of China reviewing an Honor Guard before they held talks in Beijing, June 25, 2016.

ing the war policies of the West, not simply taking up the questions of economic development, not simply developing the financial institutions like the New Development Bank and the AIIB which can replace this trans-Atlantic system, but they've actually indicated the philosophical and scientific conceptions of mankind that can secure a higher system.

And that's what I think is essential today, and this is what Mr. LaRouche has emphasized in discussions over the last couple of weeks, and especially this week, given what's developing so rapidly. So there's more to say, but perhaps there's some questions.

Question: Hello, this A— here in New York, with what may be a little bit of an update. In terms of what we're doing here in New York, specifically with the concert this Sunday that will be the beginning of a celebration of a longtime board member of the Schiller Institute, and teacher, and as I understand it—I never knew her—a genius musically: Sylvia Olden Lee.

I've been talking with people, and when you go through the strategic overview, of the threat of annihilation, and the necessary removal of Obama—all of these things—the population in my view has been really stymied and dismayed. So it becomes more clear to me each day that the flank of the beauty of music, and the ideas embedded in the works of these geniuses, become really essential for people to break their own mental bonds of slavery. So we're in a buildup now toward, to have within a year, a chorus of 1500 people, and I think this is the most significant event we're going to have so far, in terms of effect, and the depth and range of the program—the German language will be sung, Italian, the music of Handel, and Negro Spirituals. So this is a very broad program.

And I'm having fun because I'm trying to focus people on that idea of breaking through their own mental slavery, so that given things like Orlando, things like the requirement to remove Obama,— they can recognize within themselves what Lincoln called, "the better []angels of our nature." But they're so burdened,

EIRNS/Stuart Lewis

Sylvia Olden Lee at a Feb. 18-21, 1994 Schiller Institute conference music panel.

they're so bombarded that they are helpless and hopeless without doing this. And personally, from contacts that I've had before, I think, feel, and hope that this will be reflected in the attendance of people that I've talked to. Because I think I've moved them a little bit, oftentimes by using someone who has recently joined the chorus, who had first gone to the conference, attended a concert and now is a member of the chorus and having a great time doing it.

So I think the work is crucial, so that people can actually discuss everything that Dave and Mike are discussing, because I don't think people can succeed without engaging in this process.

So I wanted to raise that, and then let you elaborate on it as you see fit.

The Trans-Atlantic in Collapse

Steger: I would only add probably one thing, since I think your report stands on its own: probably one of the grossest misunderstandings we have in our society today, is the failure to understand that the natural state of the human mind is genius. That's actually the natural orientation of the human mind. As Norbert Brainin, the great musician, once said of his quartet's collaboration, "we have to resolve upward," and that the natural tendency of the mind, under optimistic circumstances, under the sense of mankind's potential for development, is to resolve upward, to resolve towards the characteristic of genius. And it really is the music work that we have concentrated on in New York, with the many choruses, with the sense of what we're inspiring within the population there, which calls us to resolve upwards, towards that quality of genius which is natural to the human species.

And it's been this artificial state of cynicism that's been imposed on people, that is really undermining what's possible today for the human species. And this is what we have to eradicate. The source of that is Obama. The key source of that cynicism, the key source of that frustration and rage, is Obama, and he has to be dismissed, flushed out of the political process. What we

EIRNS/Stuart Lewis

Violinist Norbert Brainin and pianist Günter Ludwig rehearsing for a concert dedicated to Lyndon LaRouche on Dec. 2, 1988 in Washington, D.C.

really have to do is inspire people towards something far greater than what they see is possible under the current system.

And by means of what we're doing in New York, what Kesha Rogers is doing in Houston with the space program, what we have in terms of a potential orientation towards the Pacific, this organization is really orienting the population, as best we can—we're not large; we're fairly small. But we're making clear demonstrations of what the potential of the United States is, as a nation. And that's absolutely essential, because we have to pull together a functioning government at this point. You've got to bring in a Presidency which can function. Clearly the collaborative potential with the rest of the world is increasing, and that's what we have to take advantage of.

But I think your report stands, as a significant demonstration of what we're doing.

Question: Hello, this is W—B— in Denver, and I've learned just a few hours ago that there's a plan to form a European Union army. I don't know if the LaRouche movement is aware of this yet, but this of course is very dangerous, and of course has made the war-mongers very postal [violently crazy].

But I was wondering, if there are any plans the LaRouche movement has in Western Europe

with regard to this outrageous scheme?

Steger: I think, as we see right now with the vote in Great Britain, that Western Europe is collapsing. There is an increasing pressure on the entire Atlantic Alliance, the NATO-European Union, Wall Street-London axis. This is bankrupt. Probably the best indication of this is the recent trip by Xi Jinping to Poland, even though Poland represents this kind of somewhat insane, Eastern European faction, which is getting used by this NATO program. I mean, they just placed 60,000 troops in this Baltic/Poland region, for NATO military exercises. They're beginning to bring missile defense system which are provoking us towards a greater threat of nuclear war.

But there is no capability of holding this thing together. Mr. LaRouche said in July of 2007, and this is a quote, "There is no option of a non-collapse. This system is gone." And that was regarding what was then the subprime mortgage bubble at the time. But at this point, as he said last week, this is not just a collapse of a financial system, this the collapse of an entire system, of a *whole* system.

And you see it: You see it in the general cultural

from U.S. Army video/Staff Sgt. Ricardo Hernandez Arocho

U.S. soldiers conduct a continuous fire Live Fire Exercise near Tapa, Estonia, June 20, 2016.

breakdown; you see it in Germany, you see it with the migrant crisis; you see it with the general cowardice within the political leadership. You see it in the question of the sanctions against Russia. You see that these nations of Europe cannot exist outside the New Silk Road paradigm of Russia, China, and India. They *have* to participate; their livelihood, their participation in the human species' development depends upon their moving in this direction. And their populations are facing this kind of trans-Atlantic breakdown.

Einstein's Revolution

There was a poll that came out in the United States: 81% of the American population faced difficulty paying for housing in the last five years. That should be basic! But housing prices like in the San Francisco Bay Area where I am, are over 50% of most people's income! So it's not surprising you would have problems in rent at some times, or paying your mortgage.

Creative Commons

Albert Einstein playing the violin.

So, given the level of breakdown in the United States and in Western Europe, these countries are not capable of doing this; these are pipedreams! This idea of a European army or a European resurgence, a major NATO deployment along the borders of Russia—they are tripwires; all they have is bluff. But the bluff is of nuclear war.

So the question then, is, in that context, how do we resolve it? If the trans-Atlantic region is breaking down, if it's done, if it's collapsing. There's no way it can't collapse. Look at this Presidential election: both candidates are despised by a majority of the population. You've got a breakdown in the United States. Think of the irony of what Obama calls "an economic recovery": increasing death rates, largely premised on the fact that people in their middle ages, forties and fifties—mostly white men, but predominantly white women leading the increased death rates. For the first time in decades, we have increasing rates of death. This coincides with a tripling of fatal overdoses of drugs, over just six years ago! That's within Obama's Administration, you have a tripling of people of drug overdoses in the United States. And then, just this year, you have nearly for every day of the year so far, we've had some level of mass murder.

That expresses a psychological breakdown, a cultural breakdown, far beyond just finances, the stock bubble, unemployment, and wages. This is the kind of a breakdown of a culture itself. And Obama calls that "the greatest economic recovery ever"! That's Satanic; that's not just stupidity,— that's real evil! And that's what we've got to remove.

Now, what Lyn's been raising recently, and he emphasized it today with the Policy Committee and other associates, is, you can't "describe your way into a new system." We're not talking about changing a few parts of the current economic, or political, or cultural system. To establish a culture which has true viability, long-term into the future, is not changing a few parts. It's conceiving, in a more profound and insightful way, the Universe itself, and mankind's role in it; fundamentally different than what the current society perceives.

Now, the best demonstration of this in recent contemporary history is Albert Einstein's complete revolution of science. To a large degree, Einstein's work is misunderstood,— predominantly by scientists. They don't grasp the true nature of what Einstein established. And this is clear because even during the course of Einstein's lifetime, his basic conceptions of the Universe were totally disregarded by the entire scientific establishment. He was attacked. He was personally attacked and isolated. And yet, what he demonstrated is still being verified today,— we've seen this recent demonstration of gravitational waves.

Einstein had an insight into the Universe that was fundamentally different. Where did that come from? Did Einstein come up with a mathematical equation which demonstrated what the new Universe would be like? No! That wasn't the way Einstein thought! Einstein approached his work absolutely differently. He approached it from the standpoint of how must the Universe function? The Universe must function in a more beautiful and rational way than I am currently understanding it. Because he recognized there were certain paradoxes,— that the current framework of culture did not grasp the Universe in a sufficient way to resolve the paradoxes, to resolve the contradictions. Because is it true that mankind can't advance? No! It's not true,— mankind can perpetually advance. So what's the conception of the Universe we have to go to? And Einstein developed this. And what he admits, self-consciously, is that his greatest influence at times of greatest difficulty and challenge, would be the conceptions of Mozart—the conceptions of composition that you find in Mozart's work. That that governed him!

Now, how does that work? It's much like what A— was demonstrating with the Manhattan Project and what we're doing there with the choruses and the concert this Sunday. People in the New York area, we're having a concert this Sunday on the Upper West Side that you should definitely attend. Not because it's a form of "entertainment." But it provides a demonstration, of a conception of a Universe which must govern a new economic system.

The Mission at Hand

And that's where the emphasis has to be. Because this other stuff is bluff and bluster. But that's not necessarily,— just because it's bluff and bluster doesn't mean we're saved. We're only saved if we have the courage and the creative insight to create and act upon a new and higher system. And that can only *ever* be created by the human mind. And that's really the political responsibility, that's the political fight today.

And don't count on members of Congress. They can barely get off the ground, literally. There's got to be a higher fight from a certain minority of the population who recognize that we're going to go to a higher system, and the most important factor is that you have people like Vladimir Putin who recognize what's taking place.

Putin, more than any other leadership on the planet today, recognizes that the enemy is not Western Europe, it's not the United States; it *is* the British Empire. It is a system of thought, a system of culture.

Now, how do we know that? Look at Putin's intervention into Syria. Look at over the course of the last nine months, the dramatic, fundamental changes on the planet that have been made by that intervention. And what was probably most indicative, was the concert in Palmyra. People just couldn't even comprehend it. They had helicopter escorts of Western media into this ancient, ancient amphitheater, and they held a Classical concert, and gave them a chance to see what they'd been fighting for,— a sense of real civilization. And the Western media couldn't comprehend it; they couldn't fathom what was taking place. And yet, that concert continues to resonate. The Prime Minister of Italy Renzi couldn't but help to make mention of it at the St. Petersburg economic forum.

It resonates with people, because it captures a sense of what we're actually out to accomplish as a human species, that there's a *different* conception. And that's why what Putin is doing is essential. And to the extent we operate in collaboration with that kind of creative genius, we can pull off the biggest revolution in human history. But if we don't operate this way, it'll be *our fault*. We will have failed to take the responsibility we should have.

And that should be the tension that we all have in our guts today; not just to identify the problem, but do we have the courage to go towards the solution, the optimism, the willingness to fight for something that's never been created before. And I think that's really the mission at hand.

Question: Thank's for the update. Mike, I don't want to go too far off-track. I had an organizing question for you, though, and just answer it how you feel it's fit. I keep going back to organizing around the solution: Everything I talk about, I have to remind myself not to nerd out on it, but to go towards the solution, not to get stuck in all these details, but keep it around joining the BRICS, going to the Moon, getting cold fusion, that'll solve our water problems, it'll solve a lot of job problems. And I've seen good results with it here and there, but I'm not sure how I can expand further on it. But areas I've seen good results with it on, are people who intend well, but maybe haven't had the rigor of actually doing all this—libertarians, people who are into crypto-

Margaret Greenspan

The Schiller Institute Manhattan chorus, in rehearsal with conductor Diane Sare.

currency, network computer engineers who feel that human creativity can be synthesized and therefore all the jobs can be automated and that's going to be a big problem, and we're going to be out of jobs—but keep pushing that humanity has to expand its consciousness and its creativity and get out of this planet, and therefore we will always have jobs. I've found a lot better results with that, than just spitting out facts, facts, facts, facts, facts.

And I love listening to Jeff, I absolutely love it. I love listening to all this stuff, but sometimes, for me, I feel that it distracts me from the solution. In my mind, sometimes it's not directly tied *to* the solution.

So I don't know how you can maybe help make that more clear for me. Or help us organize better around that. Or if you have a different idea. Thanks.

'How,' not 'What' You Think

Steger: I think I understand the question, of some of the facts versus a sense of the solution, but I think you answered the question. And I think you captured what's essential. I mean, there's nothing you're "supposed" to talk about. There is no formula you're supposed to abide by that's the right thing to do.

What you have to do is have—you know, Lyn has this funny reference to this German movie, "Das Spukschloss im Spessart." [The Haunted Castle in the Spessart], which is about a bunch of ghosts who come back to do their penance because they were criminals in the past. But it was done at the time when Germany was coming to terms with what the Nazi era was, and it's a comedy. And it's very light; it's meant to reawaken peo-

ple's sense that they don't have to live in the crimes of the past. That you have to live in the potential of the future. And there's a song that Lyn often references, whose refrain is *"Die Hauptsache ist der Effekt, tschike tschike tschike tschik'"* [The most important thing is the effect]. And its essence is that the main point is the effect that you have. What are you creating in the other person's mind? *That's* what you fight for. If you follow some rule, of saying, I've got to make sure they know these certain facts,— the facts may be necessary. Hopefully the facts are based on reality versus what the media's been pushing out. Sometimes truthful information is useful to at least confront people with what's happening.

But you have to be willing to engage towards a higher direction. You have to get the mind moving. You have to move them in a direction which is consistent with where the world needs to go, and you find a dialogue from that standpoint. You find a musical dialogue in that direction. And that just has to be the ongoing commitment, and that's the difficulty. It's much easier sometimes to have a formula, talk about a few facts and information or war danger, and expect that if people don't respond, they're just cowards and it's their fault, versus the idea that you can find a way of engaging people to uplift them.

And look at Lyn's approach towards the Manhattan Project: We've launched these series of choruses; we've got one in Queens, one in Brooklyn, one in Manhattan, one in New Jersey, possibly one in the Bronx. You've got a real developing of a quality of awakening the higher identity within the population. Now, what's the direct political effect of it? Well, it's creating the poten-

> That's what Einstein looked to act upon; that's what Mozart looked to act upon. Not *what* you think about the Universe; *how* you think about the Universe: To see the potential of the human mind, to see the potential of human creative insight. Because when people have that sense of capacity, then you have the ability to bring down this empire, and replace it with a true, human system.

tial of people to respond to the future! And that's the essential question. That's what we've got to accomplish.

And I think that's got to be the fight today. We do it with *urgency*, because look, we have to take this question seriously: The British Empire *is* the most evil, Satanic force on the planet. It's best expressed by the actions of Obama today. This guy has been a mass-murderer. I went through some of the facts—people know the drone references. I think up to 5,000 innocent civilians were killed by him over the last seven years. But this British Empire is Satanic.

There is a clear intent of eliminating up to 5-6 billion people from the planet. They can reduce the population by that magnitude down to approximately 1 billion people, for "governance"—to govern the population, to cull the herd. Now, this is a Satanic force. It's a historically Satanic force.

Now they are under siege. Their system is collapsing and breaking down, and not only is it collapsing and breaking down,— that was inevitable. But they have not secured the ability to bring down the entire human species. What Russia and China have done, in collaboration,— with Putin's leadership, with the developments in China now under Xi Jinping, have been remarkable. But we've got to end this tyranny. You've got to put them under siege. You have to bring down this empire. There has to be a sense of urgency. You give them a minute to breathe, and they will look to wreak havoc wherever they can.

Just look at South America: South America is now potentially on the verge of total devastation, where just a year ago, it looked like it was on the rise. Bolivia, nations that were landlocked, were looking at nuclear power, space exploration, continental rail lines. And now they're looking at a total genocide program in South America. This is the work of the British Empire, this British system. Questions of assassinations of world leaders.

Now, that's not a question of gloom and doom. It's a question of *urgency* because their system is breaking down. So we've got to bring it down, finish it. You've got the whole connection between the British, the Saudis and Obama on 9/11: *Bring them down*.

Look what the Congress just did on gun rights! They didn't follow formality, they didn't follow procedures. They basically went and shut down the entire House of Congress! Why don't they do that on the truth of 9/11? Where is the guts to take that level of responsibility?

Become More Optimistic

So we've got to bring down this British Empire, and there's got to be an urgency to do that. But then, the way the urgency expresses itself is not simply in the descriptions of what must be done, but in the method that demonstrates *how* it can be done. That we actually act upon *how* people think, not what they think. And that really is the question of genius. That's what Einstein looked to act upon; that's what Mozart looked to act upon. Not *what* you think about the Universe; *how* you think about the Universe: To see the potential of the human mind, to see the potential of human creative insight. Because when people have that sense of capacity, then you have the ability to bring down this empire, and replace it with a true, human system. And I think that's got to be the sense.

But the *urgency* and the sense of victory at this point, has to be real in people. We've got to bring this system down, and it's more possible today than it's ever been. And I think that's got to be the driving conception.

Question: Good evening Michael and Dave, this is V— in Los Angeles. Just a simple question about the way that the British Empire functions behind the curtain so to speak: I've noticed that there are a lot of very powerful, old money foundation figures like Kissinger and George Soros and these types, who are actually still quite active, they actually travel quite a lot and go to other nations and try to maybe sabotage relationships with the BRICS and things of that sort. So my simple question is, as an organization that's this small, and our forces spread thin, what kind of flanks can we use against a system which on its surface seems unbeatable?

Steger: Well, I would probably not agree with your premise; I don't know if you agree with your premise in a sense. I mean, the system is beatable: It's coming down. Shultz, Kissinger, and Soros are pathetically kind of hanging-on by a thread to the dying system that they've lived their lives enforcing, to some degree. But it's collapsing.

The modern city of Shanghai, China.

The rise of China and Russia, the development of an orientation, just the magnitude of development that we've seen now in China, but now intended for the entire area of South and Southeast Asia,— you've taken 600 million people out of poverty in China in 25 years, and you're now intending to not only replicate that within South and Southeast Asia, so that you're bringing upwards of 1.5 billion people out of poverty over the course of a 40-60 year period. You're also orienting and increasing that capacity, with a clear focus on deep-space exploration.

And this is something that—it's irrefutable that there are significant economic benefits and advancements to space exploration. That's never been denied. No one can ever make that case. They can say these are a waste of resources, which is ignorant; they're just ignorant; they don't really know. There's no competent case to make to demonstrate that space exploration has ever cost anything; it had a massive return on investment.

So why don't we do it? Well, that's exactly why you see this orientation in China, Russia, India, and the other countries involved. That is why Japan can't ignore what's taking place. Because there's something different: The system mankind must adopt, is a different conception of mankind in the Universe. And that isn't necessarily entirely clear, but the clear benefits of this orientation *are*, and unless you're dominated by a culture of cynicism, of despair, or corruption, you naturally orient in this way. The natural orientation of the mind is genius.

And that's what we've got to create now within the trans-Atlantic region. You have to create that, just as Einstein did; Einstein fought the same degeneration. He saw it firsthand throughout the course of his adult life, the kind of attacks and degeneration. But Einstein never thought it was unbeatable. He recognized clearly this thing is beatable, for the very reason that it's irrational! It's based on a lower conception of the Universe. There is a guaranteed capability to beat it, if you adopt a higher conception of the Universe,— if you adopt the conception of the Universe of Einstein, then there's no way mankind can lose.

And that's what someone like Putin has a sense of. He has a sense that it's guaranteed we can win,— as long as we can prevent them from blowing up the world, there's no way their system can continue. And that's the kind of idea that the American population urgency has to gain, is that it's winnable. But you have to go out and destroy that which is the source of evil. You can't simply appreciate the fact that good things are happening. We have to make a moral shift towards what mankind can accomplish. And I think it's just a question of the optimism; the optimism on a daily basis. People ask, "well, what can I do?"

They can become more optimistic, become more creative, become more beautiful; and then you'll find the ways by which to inspire other people, to challenge the way other people think. Take a step back from the crisis and look at the potential: How do we move the

United States upward? It's not simply by knowing the problem of the last 50 years or 70 years. You have to have a higher conception outside of that. And I think that's really the challenge, and I think people on this call may have that, but do you live up to it every day? And do you challenge other people with that conception? Because simply challenging the facts or information, will oftentimes not resolve the problem. And Einstein knew that. Einstein knew you can't simply challenge people on the facts.

The Creative Challenge

There's a famous story of Einstein, when he was asked to give a presentation on his discovery for an award,— but he just broke out his violin and played a Mozart violin sonata. Because he recognized, it's not a question of me describing to you, the Universe as now I see it; but how do I provoke a quality of thinking? And this is what Putin's engaged in; this is the Palmyra concert. But he won't repeat Palmyra; he's not going to do the same thing he's done already.

And neither can we. We constantly look for the new potentials that are taking place. Now, this Brexit vote, this vote in Europe, the collapse of the European system—regardless of which way the Brexit vote goes, this European system is collapsing, the basis of NATO is collapsing; the basis for the so-called Presidential election is collapsing. Have the media agreed to its collapse? No! But I don't expect the media to do that; but from a physical standpoint this thing's done.

The question is, what are we going to replace it with? And that's I think the scientific question we have to take up, to make sure we win.

Question: Hello, my name is N— and I'm calling from Nevada. I've only been involved with the LaRouche movement for one year, and a lot of the things that I do—I read the *Executive Intelligence Review* archives to get myself up to the same page as all of you; and I've been reading a lot about the International Monetary Fund. You wrote many articles in the 1970s and 1980s, about how they go into countries, they impose structural adjustment programs, and they leave the countries in worse shape financially. People are left with less to eat, people are starving. It just seems like they're just ruining countries.

And so, I heard that this year China was accepted into the IMF and that their currency will be part of that basket of currencies from some time in September of 2016. And my question is, when I read all of these articles in the *EIR* on the IMF, it seems like such a terrible organization with what it's doing to countries, Ibero-America, and heading our way to the U.S.A. They've got this plan, they just write up all of these numbers that aren't even correct and so forth, and loan people money.

So my question is, how come China seems to be doing the AIIB and the BRICS and they want to set up something positive, yet they want to be part of the IMF? And my second question is, when are we due for our IMF loan, when people bail out of the U.S. dollar and then we're broke—is the IMF going to come into the United States? Are we just next, the country that's going to be given austerity and so forth? Does that make any sense?

That's my question.

Steger: I think it's important to know some of the history of the fight. Probably the most important aspect is that Mr. LaRouche and our organization had pinpointed the IMF as an evil institution a long time ago. But it's fairly irrelevant now; there's no relevance to it. There's no relevance to any of these institutions—they're bankrupt, they have no significance; they have no significance in Europe.

Unfortunately, South America is facing a certain political upheaval at this point, but it can be easily turned around. I mean, the genocide practices that are now being pushed in South America could be reversed very quickly; the policies in the United States could change dramatically. One of the things Einstein recognized,— and Einstein is relevant, because this practice you're referencing from the IMF, this didn't start in the 1970s, or the 1950s or 1960s. This is a British Imperial policy that was adopted with clear intent by the late 19th Century, and formulated. And there have been direct studies, case studies on Egypt in the late 19th Century. This is partly how the Monroe Doctrine of the United States was applied to defend the nations of South America in the late 19th and early 20th Century—same practices, same colonial debt slavery that you see from the IMF.

So this is the same thing that Einstein recognized, and it's a question of how do you think about transforming the entire system. And you don't change an entire system part by part. That's why China's not worried about the IMF; you don't have to worry about these things. What you have to focus on, is what's necessary to create an entirely new system.

And this is a creative challenge. People think politics and economics are mostly facts and information,

You can't define the mathematical formula of that system, before you've developed the cultural conception of that system. It has to become an idea that resonates within a population … to bring it to bear in the minds of your population, that we're going to move upward. We're going to develop a society again. We're going to take the children born today, and over the next 25 years, we're going to develop within them a sense of creative genius, a sense of optimism, a sense of taking on the great challenges.

and do you know your facts and information?—they're not! We're talking about the actual evolutionary nature of the human species. We're not talking politics and economics as separate branches of study. These are relevant to the extent they're relevant to the human species' evolutionary development. And that evolutionary development does not take place on a step-wise basis. It's not one small step after another. Evolutionary leaps in mankind are leaps, to a higher ordering system. Einstein recognized that same characteristic, because that's how the Universe itself functions. And by intrinsic nature, if the Universe functions that way, and the mind can come to know it, then the human mind functions in a similar way.

Krafft Ehricke's Principle

This was the basis of the Italian Renaissance in the 15th Century. This was the basis of the ancient Greek Renaissance that we see with Socrates and Plato later. They captured a way of thinking. This is how mankind has made fundamental advancements in its sense of society, in its sense of humanity, and its sense of its role in the Universe. And that's the kind of quality that we now have to capture today, if we're going to create an entirely new orientation for the human species. And so, it's good. You have to know the landscape, you have to know the domain you're dealing with. You need to know this British system. But to the extent you know it, that won't be sufficient. You have to know it, because you're out to defeat it. Know your enemy, I guess, in a sense.

But we're out to create an entirely new system, independent of this enemy function, this evil practice. There are no limitations. Krafft Ehricke has a famous quote that Kesha often references, that the only limitations mankind has, are the ones that mankind places on himself. So we have no intrinsic limitations for overall growth and development. That's a different conception of the Universe than we're living in today. And we have to bring *that* kind of Universe to bear as a discovery within society!

You can't define the mathematical formula of that system, before you've developed the cultural conception of that system. It has to become an idea that resonates within a population before you can say "this is what it is, this is how we're going to measure it, this is how it's going to function." You have to bring it to bear in the minds of your population, that we're going to move upward. We're going to develop a society again. We're going to take the children born today, and over the next 25 years, we're going to develop within them a sense of creative genius, a sense of optimism, a sense of taking on the great challenges.

And that kind of commitment—and you don't have to know how we're going to do that, but you have a devotion to making the discovery and to share the discovery as it develops. And that quality of culture, that's a functioning nation, that's a functioning society. *That's* what the British Empire has been out to destroy. What the IMF system, the British system has been out to destroy is that quality of culture. They haven't just wanted to put nations into debt slavery; they wanted nations into debt slavery so they could kill the culture, so that people would not have access to this quality of development, to this quality of creative insight.

And that's what we have to generate today. So I hope that answers your question.

What is Victory?

Christie: Okay, obviously, the nature of the discussion thus far has been getting to that very idea, which is going to consistently refer to around Einstein, but clearly we're in uncharted waters, and therefore, there's no blueprint for how we proceed from here. We have a principled notion of where we've got to go. So I'm saying this is important, because people probably do have questions that they're thinking of. And I think whatever topic people have, they should just feel free to ask Mike and get a sense of clarity on the situation, or get a sense of how you might be thinking about things.

Question: Hi, it's B— in Los Angeles. I have a question on the power of the human being to be just this powerful entity of God, or the question of immortality itself. I think the question of death, which I think is the reason why people have become so susceptible to this reign of terror or whatever you want to say—it's evil—I think it's because people haven't realized the capability that we have in ourselves to be immortal, or at least to identify what that power to be a human being is.

So I think I just want to make a statement and say that, if you don't have a sense of it, I believe that people do become susceptible to becoming whatever realm of degeneracy that people may be engaged in, and I think the only way out is to learn something about oneself and this creative realm of—people reference music and poetry. But I think that people who do not engage in that obviously have not conquered the power to know what immortality is, what that sense of becoming that humanity in oneself is.

Steger: Well, take the way that—this is one way it manifests itself. You've got people in society today, who are pushed up against a wall. People are being crushed by this—it's been 15 years since the 9/11 attacks, and there's been an ongoing destruction of the country. For the first part of the G.W. Bush administration there was a housing bubble; some people had thought they had made it rich, there was a sense of maybe financial affluence. But once that blew out, you had a gross consolidation of wealth into a small percentage, and most people have been devastated ever since. There have been some pockets of increase, but in general, it's been devastated. And the terror, the horror of the ongoing perpetual war state, the constant sense of financial crisis, the constant sense of a breakdown of basic infrastructure, a breakdown of education and culture for young people, have put most people,— whether they're the young people in college today, who really have no sense at all of this, like a 19 year old who was 4 years old when 9/11 happened and grew up during this entire 15-year period, or it's the parent of that child, or the grandparent who watches both their child and grandchild suffer from consequences of either drug addiction, or cultural disorientation; so there's a real physical breakdown.

So people end up in a state of mind of desperation. And that desperation leads one to want a fundamental change, either to end it,— fine, and you hear certain people who get cynical and you hear the expression,— they don't mean it, but they say,— maybe we should just blow it up and start over. They end up toward the cynical state of mind. Because they're just so frustrated, they don't see a way out.

And when you talk to them, they also then imagine, "OK, fine, you're saying we can solve it. OK I want to solve it, I don't want to see it go to nuclear war, I don't want to see it get any worse. We've got to do something. We've got to make it better." But in their mind, they think of better as,— there's going to be a break point and it's going to "be better." And then they can keep thinking the way they've been thinking. They can keep living the way they've been living.

Well, it doesn't function that way. Because our way of thinking, our way of dealing with society on a day-to-day basis, even if it's just to endure, is not sufficient, it's not compatible with a functioning society and a functioning nation. So people want a dramatic shift, where you take away all the horror and the pain; and it's not uncommon. It's similar to people in warfare. We often talk about the post-traumatic stress disorder. People come back in a state of high anxiety and shock, and rage, because of how unjust the current system, how evil the current system is, and then the actual problems, the kind of crises that they encounter. And so you just want to "make it stop."

Now, it's not surprising that the compositions of Mozart, or of Bach, or of Beethoven, are clinically beneficial for, say, those soldiers coming back from war, as they are for a population in the state of crisis that you find the United States today. Because what you find in those compositions is a method of thinking, a conception of identity which gives one a source of strength, to actually live from day to day with a sense of optimism and of growth, a sense that "my life is going to be dedicated towards developing something." Much like a parent, if a society is at least functioning, because a parent can't raise a child, or parents can't raise a child on their own. It's the society which raises them. It's the teachers, it's the culture, it's the entertainment, it's the historical process that they're a part of. But when you have that sense, then you make those sacrifices to develop that child—it's not easy raising a child or raising a family. But you take on the endeavor, the effort, with the sense that by the time that child is 20 or 25, you now have a person in society capable of making remarkable contributions. And you take joy and pride in the fact that the society has moved upward because of your efforts. Not because your efforts were one big relief. Your efforts were still significant work, but they capture that

Winning means an opportunity to make sacrifices that now mean something, that have an immortality to them; that the contributions that we make now have an opportunity to become immortal. That my society is not reduced into need of something mortal or beast-like; but I'm going to fight for a society that appreciates the immortal contributions that the individual can make. And that's winning.

quality of tension and optimism that you get in great culture, in great composition.

And so it has to take a different quality of hypothesis. And unfortunately the emotions are so *brutish* in people today, our cultural approach towards emotions is so brutish,— because the sense of emotions is the core of an ability to make hypotheses to deal with society, to move forward. And the insights that Mozart and Beethoven have, I would say, came because they were approaching this question from the highest scientific standpoint one could—because it's not going to be that there's one great change: Glass-Steagall comes, and then wars stop, the angels sing, and now we're moving upward and everything's fine.

It's a different sense of moving a society upward, that the sacrifices people are going to make are now going to be worth something, versus the sacrifices you make today seem to make things only worse and worse. I don't think this is comprehensive by any means, but at least what I'm attempting to get at is a kind of change of identity, of how we think about what winning means. Winning means an opportunity to make sacrifices that now mean something, that have an immortality to them; that the contributions that we make now have an opportunity to become immortal. That my society is not reduced into need of something mortal or beast-like; but I'm going to fight for a society that appreciates the immortal contributions that the individual can make. And that's winning.

And that exists, that quality of "win-win" now exists on the planet, and the question is now to make that *the* dominant human culture, and to eradicate this warlike, geopolitical beast structure that the British have been imposing for far too long. It's to bring down this beast program, to bring down Obama. That's the political act to make this happen.

But this idea of what winning looks like: it's not a one final stroke, and then it's over. There's almost like a consumer mentality to that conception of winning. There's a dark age conception of winning. We need a Renaissance conception of winning, *how* we think about winning. And to the extent we actually struggle and deal with that idea, and play with it, and organize around it, then we create the foundations for a new society, a new nation.

LaRouche's 2011 Warning

Question: Hello, this is H— in New York. We have been using the shut down NATO petition, and I've gotten a report that this is also being used in Europe, in France, in Germany, and it might be useful. But we're also going to have this Warsaw summit taking place in Warsaw on July 8-9. So this is dangerous, this is time sensitive.

But the other thing I was thinking about, is we have these weapons systems that don't even work, like the famous trillion-dollar F-35 airplane—just a total waste—and how to get these people who are working on things like that to do something useful is a pretty big challenge, because we're reaching the limit. How many weapons systems can you have that cost a trillion dollars each? So that's my comment.

Steger: What's probably most interesting is that there's an increasing acknowledgment, as Dave mentioned. Dave and I were at a conference in Chinatown, San Francisco in November of 2011, when Lyndon LaRouche made a very clear forecast, that with the assassination and overthrow of Muammar Qaddafi in Libya, that there was no time. The British and Obama had no time to deal with a trial, like a Saddam Hussein trial for Qaddafi, so they basically assassinated him in the sewer, so they could move as quickly as possible, *because* of the timeframe, that they *had* to provoke a world war type scenario, or, they had to provoke a submission. They had to provoke Russia and China into an instability and submission under a British Imperial policy, and their next move was going to be Syria, because they had already set up the destabilization factors in Syria the year prior, so this was already happening. And then, the gun capacity, the military capacity, arms,

CC/Mikhail Evstafiev

A Russian Mi-8 helicopter shot down by Chechen rebels near the Chechen capital, Grozny, during the first Chechen War.

the terrorists, could move in and flood Syria for a major disruption.

And he said, "Look this is a drive towards nuclear war with Russia and China," and he made a very clear and stark warning. Lyn's been in indirect collaboration with Vladimir Putin on this idea since 1998-99, when Putin came into power and he immediately dealt with the Second Chechen War. And the First Chechen War was blown by Russia. Russia was in a complete collapse, it was shock therapy, and it was getting destroyed throughout the 1990s. And when Putin came in, he took a decisive action on the Chechen war, but he recognized, as Lyn had,— and Lyn had made very clear warnings to this network in Russia,— remember, the first place Lyn went when he came out of prison, was Russia. Putin had this orientation. And partly because of what Lyn had done with the SDI under Reagan, the SDI developments,— imagine, the SDI development was the same potential then for a fundamental change towards a global economic system as we see today; although Lyn has already made what's now possible, possible in the 1980s.

But because of British direction of the Soviet leadership, they rejected Reagan's offer of the SDI,

and plunged the world into a severe breakdown crisis by the late 1980s.

And so Lyn, immediately coming out of prison goes to Russia. By the late 1990s, he's in a dialogue with the Russian leadership around the strategic dangers of a war program, that the British are going for world war, on the premise of financial breakdown, that the bankruptcy of the West is imminent. And we've seen it: We've seen a series of breakdowns, the 1997 Asian crisis; the 1998 Russian bond crisis which almost blew out the entire Wall Street-London financial system, the so-called LTCM crisis. And you saw this breakdown ongoing throughout this last 15 years.

The Courage to Go for Victory

So Lyn recognized this danger. Obviously, we saw the same terrorist attack on 9/11, but Putin recognized it. And Russia and China today are aware of the British Imperial process. They know the enemy; Putin knows the enemy. The enemy is not the United States, the enemy is not Europe, it is the British system of outlook! It is the geopolitical system, which is archaic; it's not capable of coping with the modern developments of mankind toward space exploration. There is a statement by the head of the European Space Agency, that the day Crimea was invaded, there was a Russian, an American and a German on the International Space Station.

EIRNS/Rachel Douglas

Lyndon LaRouche addressing the memorial symposium for Pobisk Kuznetsov in Moscow, December, 2001.

Gen. (ret.) Harald Kujat, former chief of staff of the German Armed Forces, and former chairman of the NATO Military Committee.

youtube/Bananenrepublik1

U.S. Army/Visual Information Specialist Jason Johnston

Czech Republic Army Gen. Petr Pavel, chairman of the NATO Military Committee.

And so, the whole NATO structure's got to go. The whole NATO system, it's just got to go—the European Union, it's got to go. You've got to go back to a sense of collaboration among nations towards the overall development of mankind. The informal motto of NATO has been, "to keep the Germans down, Russians out, and the Americans in." And that's been the orientation.

Now, the gestures by Germany—Germany's schizophrenic at this point: It's deploying soldiers on the border of Russia, at the same time that you have an increasing grouping, the former chairman of the NATO Military Committee, Gen. Harald Kujat (ret.), and former chief of staff of the German Armed Forces, who also endorsed Steinmeier's comments that the NATO military exercises on Russia's borders are uncalled for. You had Czech Gen. Petr Pavel, who now chairs the NATO Military Committee. He came out saying there's no risk of Russia invading; there's no risk. The Bulgarian Prime Minister said there's no risk of Russia invading anyone, there's no aggressive actions. What they did in Crimea was a referendum, because the United States backed a Nazi coup; and Putin has the ability to just say this publicly—as he

did in the St. Petersburg International Economic Forum just last week—that there was a U.S. backed coup in Ukraine, so what did you expect us to do? We could have worked with a pro-Europe government in Ukraine, but the United States and NATO had to push for a Nazi coup. Putin recognizes the enemy.

And you now have Germany recognizing that they have to choose which direction they are going: Are they going with this British Imperial program, the same imperial program that governed the Hitler operation, or are they going to go with a new outlook?

And it's a conception of mankind in the Universe. So we've got to be clear on what the enemy is. The enemy is not Donald Trump, the enemy is not Hillary Clinton. They're both problems; neither of them are the solution, by any means! But the solution is to *end* this

CC/Aymayna Hyikary

Anti-government protesters in Kiev, Ukraine, attacking police troops on Feb. 18, 2014.

British system and to replace it with a system of a functioning human species on the planet. And that's what's possible today.

The alternative is a scorched-earth policy, it's what you see in South America. It's what you see in the United States, just an increasing level of destruction of the population, which ultimately will be through nuclear annihilation.

But what we see now is that it is possible to end this system. And Lyn was very clear, he was very specific on this question, so there's a reason why I make this emphasis: That we can be governed by the fear of nuclear war, but at some point you have to be willing to have the courage to go for victory, and not simply fight a war out of fear of losing, but fight to actually win, which takes a certain sacrifice, it takes a certain commitment. And it takes a different conception, because there's a responsibility in winning, to keep winning, to keep moving upward. And that's the responsibility we've got to take today.

Christie: Yes, you were discussing the NATO question, the mantra, of "keep Germany down; Russia out; the United States in," of course that's really what the issue is, really at the heart of this whole question around the European Union. Will it be the superstate, united with NATO as part of the British Empire? And to just make it clear, that statement came from Lord Ismay, who was the first NATO Secretary General. And Ismay was the top aide to Winston Churchill. Churchill was the one who set up the whole "Iron Curtain" program....

General Dynamics Astronautics

One of 20 components of a space station, Outpost, proposed here by Krafft Ehricke in 1958.

Ehricke's Conception of the Space Program

Question: Yeah, this is the anonymous R—. This is a comprehensive and really good briefing, Mike. And I'm reminded by what you just reiterated of the old canard, that the Chinese character for "crisis" is also the character for "opportunity." And I know you must be familiar with that.

The reason I'm reminded of that is because, with all this thing going on, I've had occasion to read up on Krafft Ehricke; and I found a two-volume set by him on space flight from 1960. While I was going through that, I'm learning an awful lot about just how scientifically astute this gentleman really was. I thought he was maybe a lightweight philosopher that had caught Helga's fancy or something like that. But he's truly a magnificent thinker.

And one of the things I learned is that the space program owes its origination in some degree to an oversight clause in the Versailles Treaty from 1919, where the Allies failed to restrict the German army from the development of rocketry weapons. And so there's all sorts of creative thinking that's plunged forward to make the space program reality, in a certain sense. This great, magnificent enterprise of humankind comes out of this pathetic crisis of World War I and the even more pathetic Treaty of Versailles.

So crisis can be an opportunity; and this crisis, too, could be an opportunity. And in that sense I'd like to ask you a little bit more about Krafft Ehricke's concept of mankind in space. I don't know if you need to do it in this call, but maybe somebody could write a little note on it somewhere: Krafft Ehricke versus the conception we're getting from Jeff Bezos and Elon Musk for recycling rockets and catching them on barges and making sure they land perfectly. And I think the latest story that came out was the Cape Canaveral docks were going to charge Elon Musk an extra $500 a ton to bring the reusable rockets back!

But could you talk about that, or think about that?

And another question I had is, did Ehricke ever have a correspondence with Einstein, or did Einstein ever acknowledge Ehricke in such a way that the two

> ... For Krafft Ehricke this was a leading conception: That the technology is not the question. Whether technology is good or bad, is irrelevant. The advancements in technology are critical; but the key is in the culture by which we use them; it's the cultural identification of mankind and the human species.

of those geniuses could help catalyze interest in Ehricke's vision of man's role in outer space? Because I say endorsing Ehricke would be a great thing. So that's all I've got.

Steger: What stands out with Krafft Ehricke, and some of the specific questions,— I don't know,— but I think beyond the specific question which sometimes can get an validation or an indication of things, there's something broader we can know, but often even with the right facts, people still overlook it. With Krafft Ehricke what stands out is that you had a quality of creative passion and of creative identity coming out of the early 20th Century, which you see with someone like Einstein. One of the mentors for Krafft Ehricke, Hermann Oberth was a leading figure in the space exploration program. Obviously Krafft Ehricke's outlook on space exploration was of a scientific conception of the human species which is unparalleled in science today.

And you see it similarly with people like Wilhelm Furtwängler. You take Einstein and Ehricke and you see a quality of how the creative process of the human mind is itself what shapes the political and economic endeavors of the species. And it's been someone like Krafft Ehricke, with the ability to endure the Nazi occupation that he had, which destroyed his country to a large extent, to where to continue his research and work he comes to the United States. But even here in the United States, it was clear to see the quality of destruction, as Dave just referenced, in the Churchill/Truman Iron Curtain program, which was an FBI-dominated police-state in the United States. The FBI was operating practically like the SS of the Nazis. This is an internal police state which operates from a code of conduct which is evil. And it became a dominant political force in the United States responsible for the assassinations of Kennedy, of King, the targetting of LaRouche and our organization. And when Krafft Ehricke came here, he recognized that there's a certain commitment towards space exploration, but there's not a culture which is embracing it. And even before the Apollo project was fulfilled, even before we put a man on the Moon, the pro-

gram was already getting cut. And the investments are shrinking quickly.

And five years after the landing of the Moon, he gives a presentation down at El Segundo in the aerospace sector near the airport in Los Angeles. He recognizes that there's a gross misunderstanding by many people, even people who are participating in the space program, as to what this actually is: This is a necessary course of action. It is necessary. Just as Furtwängler saw Beethoven's symphonies as necessary for mankind's advancement. To Furtwängler the music was acting upon the future of human society. He conducted the piece towards the future of human society, not towards the notes.

It's the same with Krafft Ehricke's conception of the space program, as it was Einstein's conception of what scientific thought was. Scientific thought is not a discovery of something: It's the provocation of discovery in others. The discovery one makes of any significance is a discovery of the Universe which then provokes in the minds of other scientists, further discoveries. What Einstein was attacked by was a cult, a cult set up by Bertrand Russell, but a cult of mathematics which said that discoveries can no longer be made. And that's the same culture which came to dominate the space program environment.

That's What We Must Fight For

And so Krafft Ehricke took on the problem of the environmentalists. So he took on Nazis, then he took on the fascists in the FBI, who basically began to dismantle the space program after they killed Kennedy and then killed his brother Bobby, and then, he took on the environmentalist movement, which was really just one more aspect of the same kind of breakdown of this trans-Atlantic British system. And he recognized that question, and what he loved about his work with Helga and Lyn was that they recognized it, and for Krafft Ehricke this was a leading conception: That the technology is not the question. Whether technology is good or bad, is irrelevant. The advancements in technology are critical; but the key is in the culture by which we use them; it's the cultural identification of mankind and the human species.

And that's not something that you can provoke within a society by a description. Deductions will fail You can't deduce in the minds of a people, or through education, you can't deduce in the minds of young people what the proper orientation of human identity is. You can't conclude it by logical argument. You can't define it by some formula that this is what human existence is. Because it doesn't exist that way!

Once you define it that way, you kill human identity! And this was why Krafft Ehricke loved what we were doing as a political movement. And if only he had lived, if only he hadn't been plagued by some of these illnesses. He was dedicating himself to this direction. And there was that same passion he had to oppose the Nazis, to oppose the FBI, to oppose the green agenda, that he recognized in what we were providing as a means, a social movement by which you could overcome these problems, because you needed a movement to provoke a sense of discovery, and not just *a* discovery, but the *method* of discovery: The means by which discovery is made or the domain from which discovery is made.

And that really is what we have to fight for. That's the kind of culture that Einstein and Krafft Ehricke fought for, and that really is what the new system of human economic value has to be: the potential to provoke further discovery in the future, to provoke others to take on the great challenges. That's not a "fact"; that's not a discovery, or it's certainly not any kind of equation of something.

So that's what Krafft Ehricke and Einstein shared, and this is very clear, and this is what Lyn captures today. That's why Lyn's such a dominant political force on the planet, today, because of this quality. Why? Because it's a higher quality of thinking. It's more rational. It's more beautiful, for Einstein as for John Keats, the poet: Beauty is an indication of truth in the Universe. And that's what Lyn recognizes. He recognizes that we have more power in the Universe today if we attain this quality of thinking, if we dedicate ourselves to this quality of thinking. And that's what gives us the basis, but it's also the basis by which we can establish a new system. They're the means and the end.

And I think that kind of conception is what has governed all geniuses throughout human history, that quality, that sense of understanding. And what we don't want to do, is resolve down. Resolved? Yes, okay, that's true, but we have to resolve to something lower, something

more comprehensible, something more that people will understand. Well that's just pessimistic! People won't understand their own creative potential? Why wouldn't they? Why wouldn't they love it? Isn't it a sense of freedom? Isn't it a sense of awe about the mind's ability to penetrate the way the Universe functions?

I think people are capable and want to. This is an intrinsic desire within every individual to grasp that sense of creative genius. But there also has to be a dedication, a quality of leadership to provoke it and that's what's absolutely essential today.

Enjoy This Moment

Question: This is T— from Virginia. Thanks again Mike for going through everything, the current situation with culture and how that's a necessity, because it pertains to my question. When I'm talking to people about all these great solutions attributed to Mr. LaRouche, the Silk Road, the new paradigm, BRICS, the space program, all these things look good on paper. The people agree, but you know, they're not going to fight and they support and they do everything contrary to what they say they agree with.

So of course, when you're speaking of the culture, and how it's taking precedence and its shaped these types of responses, I get why people simply agree and do nothing. The culture now is really repulsive, and on top of that, you can barely even recognize how bad things are with the drugs.

For me personally, the Classical music is what works for me; and had I not picked up playing the flute again two years ago, I probably wouldn't be on this call! And you just mentioned how Mr. LaRouche always points out Classical music as being a necessity to move people forward, to move them into the Hamiltonian system, and aligning the BRICS and all these great things. My question is, how can I approach people with the idea of embracing Classical music and Classical culture without them interpreting it as just another one of these great things that my movement does, and they'll just simply agree to it?

Steger: Well, there's no timeframe. You're dealing with a physical process. There's an intrinsic time, but with each person that's going to be somewhat different, so you can't predefine It. You can't predefine: this person hasn't made it so I guess they won't. You don't know. So the question is, do you just enjoy the provocation and the delight in the discussion of these ideas? And that's like you said: in participating in a musical

Xinhua/Liu Weibing

Chinese President Xi Jinping (standing) addresses the welcome banquet held by Polish President Andrzej Duda (third from right, rear) in Warsaw Poland, on June 20, 2016.

process, it keeps your mind alive and elevated, that you're resolving upwards. And that really is the endeavor.

You know, when Lyn gets these kinds of questions, his answer is, well, look what I'm doing. And you have to: He's 93 years old, his movement has been torn to pieces,— you can imagine, our organization was taken over by an ideology and FBI kind of operation when Lyn was in prison.

So they put him in prison, unjustly for five years, at the time the entire system was coming down. He's the only economist on the block so to speak, to forecast the end of the Soviet system and the fall of the Berlin Wall. Helga—everyone, all of the leadership of the organization as they describe it, were shocked when Lyn said, the Berlin Wall is coming down.

It's ironic that the President of China said "We should make Poland the example for all of Europe," recently on his trip to Poland just the end of last week. They're developing a whole port and transit logistics system in Poland, and integrating Poland to be a key pathway of the main rail corridor from China, from Chongqing in central China to Duisburg, the main inland port on the Rhine, in Germany. But Lyndon had said the same thing: He said give me Poland; let Poland be an example of a collaborative effort towards development between both the former Comecon system [Soviet-Eastern European

economic bloc] and Western Europe, and let Poland be an example of where Europe can go.

Now, Lyn was put in prison at that point. He was *in prison* when the Wall came down!

And so, the FBI largely took over the organization. And they ran all kinds of disruptions. What was the main attack they had? The main attack on the organization was to lose the joy of provoking the process of creative discovery. Turn it into something analytical. Turn it into something where we can do this, and this, and this, and then somehow we'll get the political break we need. You reduce it to some kind of mathematical equation; you reduce it to some kind of analytical tactics. You lose the actual process. You reduce it to the constant crisis in money, because you're facing an economic breakdown.

Versus recognizing you've got to provoke a quality of creative discovery in others, and there has to be a sense of joy in that fight. You're dealing with a breakdown of the entire British Empire, British System. This is not the breakdown of a housing bubble. As Lyn has compared it before, this is like the breakdown of the Roman Empire, when following that collapse, there ensued a Dark Age for hundreds of years.

Our efforts are to avoid a Dark Age that could potentially threaten to consume mankind with a Dark Age for hundreds of years, if not a kind of Apocalyptic Dark Age of nuclear annihilation.

To really enjoy, that's the question. We're not trying to stop losing. You have to look for the conception of victory. [Nicholas of] Cusa has this conception of the "not-other." Because it's not other than not-other; it is that which is good. You have to identify and develop that conception. You can't simply say, "I want to stop losing." You can't define it negatively. And you can't necessarily impose on people *when* they're going to make the discovery. Oftentimes when you do that, when we expect people to make a discovery at a certain timeframe, it only drags the process down, because we're not really enjoying, we ourselves are not participating in the creative process.

We're saying, "Look, you've got to do this," because … you're going to put in some arbitrary expectation on them, versus just enjoy provoking their mind and see how they respond. What you will find is that people get it, because it's not an analytical process that we're asking them to understand. It's a sense of freedom. With most people today, in this culture, with this entertainment, with this news service, with this education, with this traffic, and the kind of work that people are engaged in, or the family lives that are so broken down, the freedom of the mind is not there.

And so, I think we just have to enjoy it. As Lyn says, look at him. Look at how Lyn's operating. Enjoy this moment. We have the potential today to achieve a great victory, if we recognize the sense of urgency to crush this system, to bring down Obama, to bring down Wall Street. We're not looking for reform, we're looking for the elimination of this Wall Street/London system. We're looking to bring down Obama, to bring down this whole Presidential fraud.

Awaken This in People

People say, "How are you going to do it?" *It's happening!* It's happening because of what Putin and China and most of the human species right now is participating it. This is an undeniable advancement of the human species. It's challenging the bankruptcy of the trans-Atlantic system. As Einstein knew, when the system changes, it's the whole system. You can't change it in parts. It's the whole process.

I want to address your particular question, but I would point to that way of thinking, the way Lyn approaches it, the kind of fight Lyn's taken on—he's rebuilt his organization within the last two years, with the orientation in Manhattan, and then with Kesha's revival of the space program, with what Dave and I are doing on the West Coast regarding Russia and China and the Pacific orientation, we have reoriented,— leading with Manhattan, leading with the revival of this kind of choral principle, we have recreated,— he has recreated his organization. It took him 20 years, after coming out of prison, but he has recreated it at a critical juncture in the political process.

That's a quality of devotion. That quality of action by Lyn inspires me every day—to not worry if other people are making the discovery on the timeframe that they should be. My sense of urgency is to continue to provoke other people, whoever they might be, to make that discovery. And that's why Lyn's such a leading figure today.

Christie: We have a few people left in the queue. Do you want to take another question or two?

Steger: Yes, if there's two more, why don't we take those two questions?

Question: Hi! This is D— in Wisconsin. I unfortunately missed the first hour. I'm wondering, you guys may have already answered it, the impotent sit-in by the Congressional Democrats over that gun issue the last 24 hours?

Steger: Yeah, we touched on it and I think you just made the point. This is pathetic and they've chosen to become irrelevant. The question is, how relevant are we? They show what irrelevance looks like. I think that's pretty clear. So now, what are we going to do? How are we going to operate in this kind of unique historical moment? That's what's got to govern our sense of a process. That's what I would say.

Question: Hi! This is I— from Brooklyn. Forgive me Mike and Dave, but I just want to thank you for being spot on. My question is, to what degree and extent would you categorize the strength of the British system as the ghost? How could we de-mask the ghost? What are their strengths, especially culturally and financially? To what extent do they influence the average citizen?

You guys mentioned the ghost that Mr. Lyn was talking about, the movie ["Das Spukschloss im Spessart"—The Haunted Castle in the Spessart]. I was just using that as a metaphor in order to sort of understand how the British system affects how a citizen understands the current reality that he is in. In other words, how would you characterize the strength, institutionally, as far as poverty-wise, and culturally, as well as financially? How was the British system able to transform the political, economic, and industrial history of the American system? Was it done consciously, or was it just accepted subconsciously?

Steger: Okay. I think I get the question. This [German] movie that Lyn references, I think we posted a fairly good version of it on YouTube with [English] subtitles. There's a quality of joy that's possible within human life, and it's that which we have to unleash in the American people. People have been crushed under a society which has replaced joy, towards a banal kind of pleasure. They think of the banal pleasure as a way of escaping the torture of the current society.

The new issue of *EIR* magazine is out this week. In the back of it there is a presentation from the Saturday

> ... Young people brainwashed on this environmentalism, brainwashed on the obsession with recycling, this obsession of concern with the Earth. If you really are concerned, then you have to approach the challenges of space exploration, which don't require constipated worry. They require a playfulness of human creative thought ... They require real philosophical insight, a real imagination, and a lot of incredibly challenging, long, focused, concentrated work—real work, towards what we can accomplish with this imagination and potential.

[June 18] Manhattan discussion that John Sigerson provided. He references this Orlando massacre. These are 20-, 22-, 25-year-old young people. They are in some dark, kind of unlit, horrible—it's like a hell-hole. Why are they there? To escape the insanity of society? You run to something like that, to find some escape?

There's a loss of a sense of real joy. The means by which you awaken that sometimes is very playful, as this movie is that they did in Germany in the 1960s, where they really make it clear that most of West Germany is run by a bunch of British and CIA spies, who basically are no different from the Nazis [laughs], so you have to have a certain sense of humor, that what the Nazis were, wasn't something necessarily that just had a goose-step and a swastika.

You have to awaken a sense of playfulness in people. It's the same with all these young people brainwashed on this environmentalism, brainwashed on the obsession with recycling, or whatever, this obsession of concern with the Earth. If you really are concerned, then you have to approach the challenges of space exploration, which don't require constipated worry. They require a playfulness of human creative thought: How do we solve these great challenges of space exploration? They require real philosophical insight, a real imagination, and a lot of incredibly challenging, long, focused, concentrated work—real work, towards what we can accomplish with this imagination and potential.

I think we've just got to awaken that in people. Awaken a sense of *joy* of what it means to be human and participate in a society that's focused and oriented towards accomplishing such goals, and that we can say today that there exists, on this planet, that focus. You'll see it manifest this weekend. There is a focus on the planet, increasingly, towards this quality of the human species, and we should take great joy in that, and recognize with that comes a real sense of responsibility to ensure that it continues.

The best way to ensure that is to get rid of this creep Obama, to get rid of this British system, and to focus on that kind of higher conception of mankind. The sense of joy and playfulness is irreplaceable. It really is the heart and soul of Mozart and Beethoven. As intense as their compositions are, the playfulness is ever-present.

Christie: Okay. I think we're going to call it there. We have a few of our long-time allies left in the queue, but feel free to call Mike on any questions you may have. I very much appreciated the discussion so far this evening. I can only just say this: tune in to LaRouche PAC this weekend. The quality of intervention we are making this weekend is really unprecedented. The timing of where we're at is unprecedented. We know that no matter what has happened with the situation around the Brexit [vote], clearly it's doomed no matter what. But as a kind of a shock, at least at this point, with about half of the votes counted, the "Leave" campaign is up by about 500,000 votes. It's tight still. They're only up to 51.7%, but obviously the implications of this are going to be tectonic either way. The leadership to guide humanity out of this crisis is being provided by Putin this weekend over what he's doing with China, the ongoing meetings with the SCO, and what he's done since the St. Petersburg International Economic Forum, but also what Lyn and Helga are up to this weekend. People should just absolutely tune in, pay attention, especially to the webcast tomorrow, which will include input from both Helga and Lyndon LaRouche.

So, yeah, stay tuned. Mike, I don't know if you have any final thoughts here, but if you do, why don't you lay them out.

Steger: I think, people, we should have some fun and get to work. There's a lot to do!

Christie: Okay. That sounds good. Thanks for joining us this evening. Like I say, stay tuned this weekend. Bye!